THE BATTLE OF
Gettysburg
1-3 JULY 1863

Written and illustrated by

IAN RIBBONS

London
OXFORD UNIVERSITY PRESS
1974

OXFORD UNIVERSITY PRESS, ELY HOUSE, LONDON W.1   GLASGOW   NEW YORK   TORONTO   MELBOURNE   WELLINGTON   CAPE TOWN   IBADAN   NAIROBI   DAR ES SALAAM   LUSAKA   ADDIS ABABA
DELHI   BOMBAY   CALCUTTA   MADRAS   KARACHI   LAHORE   DACCA   KUALA LUMPUR   SINGAPORE   HONG KONG   TOKYO   ISBN 0 19 273125 4 © IAN RIBBONS 1974   FIRST PUBLISHED 1974</br>
PRINTED IN AUSTRIA

The Greatest Civil War in History

is at its height. For two years fighting has spread; now, from Virginia to California, across a territory almost the size of Europe, men of one nation are locked in conflict. The United States of America is torn apart, South against North, North against South.

In Tennessee, Mississippi, Virginia, Pennsylvania, troops are marching, some blue-clad, some in grey. Officers who trained as cadets together at West Point find themselves enemies in battle. Mothers have seen one son depart to fight for the North, another, bitterly opposed, to enlist for the South.

Land is scarred, farms ruined, towns shattered, railways and bridges destroyed. Plantations stand deserted. Carolina's coast is blockaded; on the Mississippi River a whole city is starving, besieged. In the path of oncoming enemy troops, families have left homes and possessions, fleeing by wagon as refugees bound for an alien land.

Each side is convinced utterly of its cause: the South of its struggle for liberty, of its right to independence; the North of its duty to crush rebellion which threatens the Union. For everyone the future of the Republic is at stake, a decision whether America shall be one nation or two. Bitterness has reached depths undreamed of when war began. Newspapers report atrocities—usually exaggerated—and clamour for vengeance.

Battles are fought with murderous loss. This summer, among the splintered tree stumps of Malvern Hill and in the matted wilderness of Chancellorsville, bones of soldiers, still unburied, whiten in the sun. During some weeks the trains jolted daily into the rail depots of Richmond and Washington to unload their grim cargoes of wounded. Beyond the war zone, Baltimore has hotels and citizens split into rival factions who barely speak.

The long war is both at its mid-point and at its climax. These few coming days will decide its course. In the west, two southern bastions on the Mississippi are the last barriers to a northern advance downriver to New Orleans. To the east, a sudden thrust by the main army of the South has penetrated deep into northern territory to within 80 miles of Philadelphia. Lean men in grey are tramping out from a mountain pass into open farm country; choking in the dust of turnpike roads, a northern host is moving by forced marches up through Maryland to meet them. By a road junction between cluster the spires and trees of a quiet country town, centre of Adams County, Pennsylvania. Here, among hills and fields and woods encircling the spot, the most momentous battle of the war is set.

Maps show the town's name as Gettysburg.

Differences

174 years after the first English Colony of Virginia was settled in Chesapeake Bay, the American Colonies won Independence from the British and, 6 years later, declared a free Federation of the United States. Two further vast tracts of land were acquired; in 1803 the Mississippi Basin, the "Louisiana Purchase", from France, and later, from Mexico, the whole south-west of the continent, from Texas to California. Settlers followed the land, spreading westwards.

Since the U.S.A. became a nation, the ways of life of North and South have drifted apart. To a booming population in Europe the northern and western states beckoned as a country of unlimited promise, luring wave after wave of immigrants across the Atlantic to a better life. Machinery to till vast wheatlands and to build iron foundries followed. The North became powerful, industrial, New York a world business centre.

But in a rapidly changing world, the South remained agricultural. Needing to import its machine goods, it depended for prosperity mainly on rice and cotton grown in the deep South, exporting raw cotton to the textile mills of England and Europe. It was a land of family estates, worked for generations by Negro slaves.

Above all the South was proud. Virginia was the oldest state in the Union; it had provided 6 Presidents. Southern aristocrats had for half a century dominated the Federal government at Washington. Many Louisianan families carried the traditions of pre-Revolutionary France. The southern landowner, whether paternal or tyrant, was a "gentleman". Now he saw the South losing power everywhere to the North. Immigrants swelled northern cities and farms. The South no longer dominated the Federal Government; the North was becoming richer every day. Feelings blinded judgement. The Southerner saw the northern mill owner as a self-made upstart, profiteering on cheap Irish labour, without a thought beyond money. The Northerner saw the southern planter as a dandy who sat on a verandah, watching his slaves.

And under every difference simmered the most emotional issue of all, slavery.

The earliest Colonists had held slaves, but the system had mostly died out in the North. Smaller farms and colder winters in New England made it uneconomic, anyway. The southern aristocrat, however, had owned slaves all his life. Even the Constitution recognized slavery, although it forbade it in all new territory north of the Ohio River. The lands of the Louisiana Purchase carried slaves; when Louisiana was admitted to the Union as a slave state, neighbouring Missouri, although beyond the Ohio, was allowed to keep slavery too. To balance this, all other land lying north of Missouri's southern boundary was to be forever "free". In states created from lands surrendered by Mexico settlers were given "squatter sovereignty" to choose for themselves.

Most educated men, in both North and South, believed in eventual emancipation of the Negro, but northern abolitionists campaigned for immediate freedom of all slaves everywhere. Southern extremists sought a Federal decree making slavery permanent.

Violence flared when, in 1854, the new states of Kansas and Nebraska, although both *north* of the Missouri line, were given squatter rights of choice. Agitators from both sides poured into Kansas. The town of Lawrence was sacked by a pro-slavery mob; in reprisal an abolitionist gang, led by a fanatic called John Brown, murdered 5 pro-slavery settlers.

Brown worked and planned to arm a slave uprising, and in 1859 attempted to seize the government arsenal at Harper's Ferry. Brown was hanged, reviled by the South as a ruffian, but revered by northern abolitionists, chanting "John Brown's body", as a saint. In the face of incitement to bloodshed, even moderate Southerners began regarding the North as an enemy. And if the new Republican party, containing many abolitionists, came to power, as seemed likely, the future for the South would look dark indeed.

For years Southerners had talked of "secession". Southern lawyers held that, as states had freely joined the Union, they were equally free to leave it. Finally, on 20 December 1860, South Carolina voted to cut loose. Within 5 weeks Mississippi, Florida, Alabama, Georgia, Louisiana and finally Texas followed, and on 18 February 1861 delegates met at Montgomery, Alabama, to swear in Jefferson Davis as President of the new Confederate States of America.

Davis was 55, Kentucky born, conspicuous when a young officer in the Mexican war, 4 years U.S. Secretary of War, late Senator for Mississippi. For a soldier, he spoke calmly, only of defence.

Two weeks later, in Washington, Abraham Lincoln, leader of the victorious Republican party, was inaugurated President of the U.S.A. Like Davis he used restrained words, promising the South it would not be attacked. But he added a footnote: as he considered the Union still in force, Union authorities were empowered to "hold, occupy, and possess" government property lying within various states.

And square in Charleston harbour, $3\frac{1}{2}$ miles from the capital of South Carolina, lay Fort Sumter. A Union garrison of some 70 soldiers under Major Anderson had abandoned their mainland forts, moved into Sumter, and with 48 guns dominated any approach by sea. Charleston Confederates, furiously demanding Anderson's surrender, began building shore batteries opposite the fort. Supplies were stopped and a food ship sent by Washington turned back before it could reach the inner channel.

U.S.A.

Territories
Washington Territory
Montana Territory
Dakota Territory
Utah Territory
Colorado Territory
Arizona Territory
New Mexico Territory

Northern States

OREGON
MINNESOTA
WISCONSIN
MICHIGAN
NEW YORK
VERMONT
NEW HAMPSHIRE
MAINE
CALIFORNIA
KANSAS
IOWA

MISSOURI
ILLINOIS
INDIANA
KENTUCKY
OHIO
PENNSYLVANIA
MARYLAND
DELAWARE
NEW JERSEY
CONNECTICUT
MASSACHUSETTS

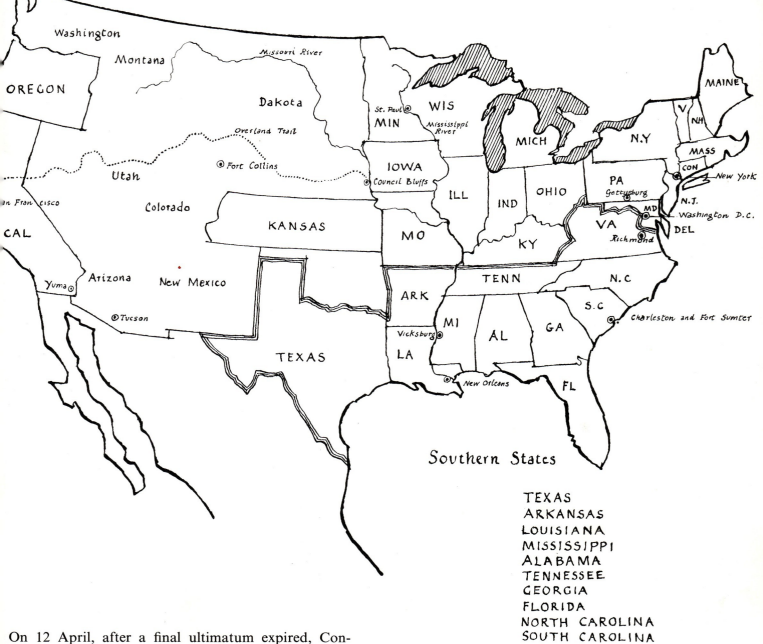

Southern States

TEXAS
ARKANSAS
LOUISIANA
MISSISSIPPI
ALABAMA
TENNESSEE
GEORGIA
FLORIDA
NORTH CAROLINA
SOUTH CAROLINA
VIRGINIA

On 12 April, after a final ultimatum expired, Confederates opened fire on the fort. Anderson, hopelessly outgunned, surrendered 2 days later. Armed rebellion was a fact.

War

The news of Sumter's surrender was received with frantic cheers and with much foreboding, but the weight of decision lay on Abraham Lincoln. South Carolina had seized U.S. property by force; if this were tolerated, Carolina's independence, and with it that of the Confederacy, would be as good as won. Recognition by a sympathetic England and France would surely follow.

Lincoln, the awkward backwoodsman, born one year later than Davis in the same state of Kentucky, and small town lawyer, was no career politician. But directness, honesty, earthy common-sense, and natural eloquence had made him spokesman for his party. Now, in a crisis situation which had no rules, he had to feel his way.

He was certain perhaps of one thing, a passionate belief in the destiny of the American nation, in the binding contract of Union. Beyond hatred of slavery, beyond any rivalry between states, he saw his paramount duty as that of saving the Republic.

The means to do this, in 1861, were pitifully thin. The regular U.S. army, only 12,000 men, was scattered in far-off Texas. Washington was surrounded by southern sympathizers and unguarded. Lincoln had to act swiftly or not at all.

One day after Sumter fell, he called on all loyal states to provide 75,000 volunteer militiamen, signing for 3

months' service, to deal with "combinations too powerful to be suppressed" by police or marshals. Virginia, outraged at being asked to take arms against sister states, and North Carolina and Arkansas, about to secede anyway, joined the Confederacy. The border states of Kentucky, Tennessee, Maryland also refused troops but kept uneasy neutrality. The first militia to reach Washington, the 6th Massachusetts, was stoned in the streets of Baltimore while marching between rail depots; following regiments found bridges destroyed by citizens. For some days the capital was cut off from the North and open to capture.

In the opening campaigns, initiative lay with the South. Southerners, mostly bred to arms, despised the city clerks and farmers of northern armies as rabble.

The struggle divided into 3 theatres: the Mississippi valley in the west, Kentucky and Tennessee in the centre, and, most important of all, Virginia in the east. Richmond, as capital of its most powerful state of Virginia and nearest the battle-front, became also capital of the Confederacy.

After a year's fighting, huge northern resources in men, weapons, ships, manufacturing, began to tell. Coast blockade crippled the South's overseas trade; Union troops (now called Federals) took New Orleans; a large Federal army threatened Richmond.

But the Confederacy held one enormous advantage, as yet unused. An ex-colonel of U.S. Engineers, with an uncanny eye for judging terrain and visualizing troop movements, with the highest reputation for boldness and determination under fire, who had actually refused command of the whole U.S. army before war broke out, sat cooling his heels in an office as Davis's War Advisor. Robert E. Lee, now General, was the most eminent soldier in North America. When Virginia had seceded, he had resigned his U.S. commission to serve the state of his birth.

In the spring of 1862 the defences before Richmond were crumbling. Taking field command of a disorganized army in the middle of battle, outnumbered and on the verge of defeat, Lee welded the pieces and by daring and speed won a masterly campaign of 7 days in June. Pressing on, he invaded the North, but was checked bloodily at Antietam. Back on the defensive he outmanoeuvred a stronger enemy to win 2 more crushing victories, at Fredericksburg and Chancellorsville. Forged by Lee in battle conditions, the Confederate Army of Northern Virginia was by now the most formidable force in the world.

But Virginia was only one front. Sea blockade held; pushing west, Federal troops had reached the Mississippi and threatened a downriver advance to cut the South in two; a massive, rebuilt Federal Army of the Potomac lined the Rappahannock 50 miles from Richmond. And, not least, Lincoln had seized the occasion of a northern near-victory at Antietam to proclaim that all slaves in captured territory would be freed. This move gave the northern war effort the colour of a crusade, swaying public opinion in Europe and killing any chance of armed help from there to the South.

Lee's veterans lacked horses, clothing, food, numbers. And his greatest general, "Stonewall" Jackson, was dead, shot accidentally by his own men at Chancellorsville. By May 1863, Davis realized supreme crisis was at hand.

What neither Davis nor Lee knew was that the unstable Joe Hooker, who had boasted that his Federal army had Lee's in its pocket, was, since his rout at Chancellorsville, already a marked man in the inner councils of the U.S. War Department. A very different general was soon to take his place.

As yet unaware of his stars, a tough bespectacled Pennsylvanian, known to his hard-driven troops in V corps as "Ol' Snapping Turtle", was destined to command the Army of the Potomac in its most desperate battle of the war. He was George Gordon Meade.

Invasion

In mid-May, Lee went to Richmond. After long discussions, Davis approved Lee's plans for a second invasion of the North. If Lee's army could secretly strike camp, slip past the Federal army in its front, raid deep into Pennsylvania to menace Washington, New York and the rail links to Harrisburg, it could draw off enemy pressure from Richmond and spread civilian panic which might lead to northern overtures for peace. Lee's men could capture all the beef cattle, cavalry horses and supplies they so badly needed, and if forced to major battle they should hold the initiative.

Without Jackson now, Lee reformed his infantry in 3 corps: 1st under General James Longstreet; 2nd under General Richard Ewell: 3rd under General A. P. Hill. Each corps was 20,000 strong, with its own artillery. One would cross west behind the shield of the Blue Ridge mountains, march north-east through the Shenandoah and Cumberland valleys, recross the mountains near Cashtown and cut through the heart of Pennsylvania towards Harrisburg. Another corps, marching east of the Blue Ridge, would act as cover for the last to follow the first, before crossing the mountains as rearguard. Eastwards a mobile screen of cavalry would cut railroads and harass the Federal rear, keeping contact with and finally rejoining the main army.

Ewell marched first. Through early June his columns, safely threading the mountain pass of Chester Gap, moved steadily up the valley. Capturing Winchester, they reached the Potomac on the 22nd, waded the river at Williamsport, crossed the neck of Maryland into Pennsylvania, and, continuing fast northwards, occupied Chambersburg on the 24th. That day Lee with the 2 rear corps stood poised on the south bank of the Potomac crossings. The next, the 25th, ladies in coaches on the Maryland bank had a fine view of some of the 40,000 soldiers who "waded . . . hip deep most men took off all their clothing carrying them . . . on their shoulders . . . a lively seen" noted Sgt. Vairin. "Here we are, ladies, as rough and ragged as ever . . ." shouted one veteran.

After war-ravaged Virginia, the army marched into another world: huge barns, cosy towns, ripening wheat. "We pressed everything . . . flour corn malasses whiskey clothes cattle horses . . ." wrote Lt. Boatwright. Goods were strictly paid for, but farmers and townspeople looked sourly at Confederate money.

The army appeared odd itself. A dry goods merchant in Chambersburg saw "dress . . . of nearly every . . . colour and style . . . skeletons of what had once been hats . . . ragged, shoeless, and filthy". Citizens were awed, though, by the bronzed, disciplined ranks marching silently, rifles gleaming.

On Friday the 26th Ewell's leading division, under General Jubal Early, crossed South Mountain, swept through Greenwood—smashing an iron works—seized 2,000 food rations from Gettysburg rail depot and burned 12 wagons. Saturday the men marched east, burning all wooden bridges along the line of the new railroad as far as Hanover Junction, thence along the Northern Central towards York. Sunday 28 June found them stranded at Wrightsville before a Federal-destroyed bridge over the Susquehanna.

With his main force now at Chambersburg, Lee had one unforeseen, gnawing worry. Never before had General J. E. B. Stuart's hard-riding squadrons, the army's cavalry "eyes", failed to report constantly and fully the position of an enemy. But since the 23rd they had not been seen or heard from. Their advance guard should actually have rejoined Ewell by now; not one message had been received. Lee could only hope, uneasily, that their silence meant the Federals were still sitting on the Rappahannock.

That Sunday night a travel-worn spy gained Lee's camp, bearing staggering news. The whole Federal army had crossed the Potomac and was marching north, one wing already near South Mountain, able to cross and cut Lee's line of communication down the Cumberland Valley.

It would be a race against disaster. Invasion must be halted, Lee's scattered army must concentrate, and gain room to manoeuvre in open country. Within hours new orders were drafted and away. Ewell's corps to retreat south, the other two to thread the mountain pass eastwards by the Cashtown road, all to meet near Gettysburg.

The next evening, from the Reform Church steeple in Chambersburg, Jacob Hoke saw signal lights "for miles up and down the valley". At night a "low rumbling" came "through the half-closed shutters . . . a continuous stream of wagons . . . turning east at the Public Square . . . out on the Gettysburg pike". They could only be following a Confederate army eastwards.

At daylight a warning was scribbled to the state government at Harrisburg. Stephen Pomeroy, changing horses, rode a 15 hour detour, evaded enemy pickets and gained the telegraph office at Port Royal.

By the 29th, Pennsylvania was in ferment. General Couch at Harrisburg telegraphed: "My whole force is perhaps 16,000 men . . . 5,000 regulars will whip them all to pieces . . ." Northern news correspondents raced to catch up the Union army, known now to be moving, and expected battle. Whitelaw Reid found Washington "like a city besieged . . . All night long, troops . . . marching; orderlies with clanking sabres . . ." Baltimore's streets were barricaded with tar-barrels. Frederick, on Tuesday night, was "Pandemonium . . . liquor shops are in full blast". Army H.Q. was rumoured at West-

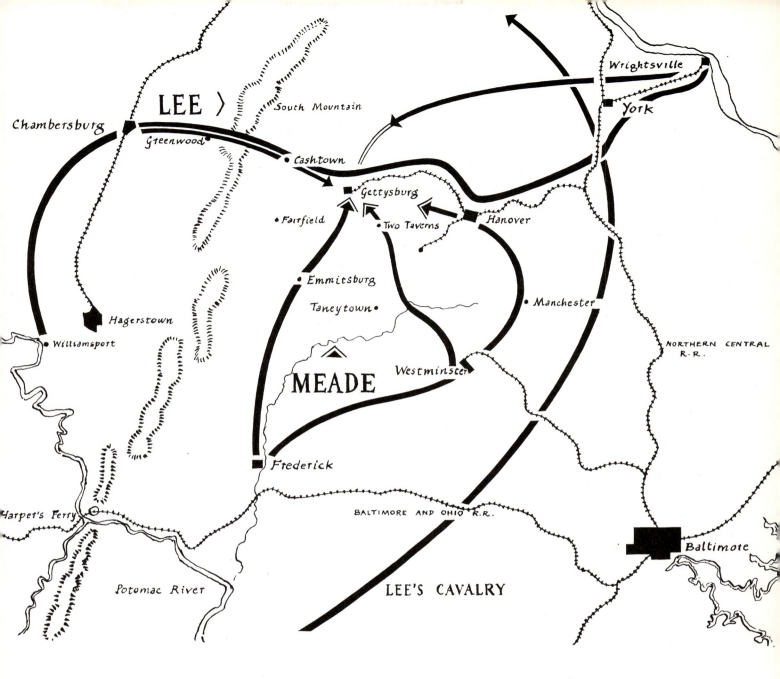

minster; with no further railroute Reid bought a horse to ride overland.

By Tuesday, Federal Army H.Q. actually reached Taneytown. General George Meade, promoted to army commander only 3 days before, thought, from what reports he had had, that Lee's main force was still beyond the mountains, westwards. Meade's 7 army corps, each about half the size of Lee's, were fanning out of Frederick by forced marches on diverging roads, ready to concentrate the instant one struck the enemy. Farthest north, General John Buford's cavalry division had advanced beyond the road junction of Gettysburg to screen the Chambersburg pike, a mile west of town. Southwards, General John Reynolds was leading the élite I corps up from Emmitsburg; XI and III corps were following behind, all three making the left wing of Meade's army.

All Tuesday Confederate troops tramped South Mountain in rain. The leading division, under General Henry Heth, was already in the Cashtown pass. Heth's men needed shoes, and the country town of Gettysburg they could see below looked a likely place to find them. A reconnaissance spied Buford's blue-coats and reported the sound of drums. Hill's corps H.Q., however, assured Heth that any Federals ahead could only be scouts—Meade was thought to be miles southward—and gave permission to enter Gettysburg the next morning for the shoes.

Buford's cavalry, meanwhile, had reported sighting men in Confederate grey. Buford sent a courier galloping to Meade; before midnight the whole Union army was ordered to march at dawn and to converge cautiously on the area. Somewhere to the south, two telegraph boys were riding through the night with a telegram which reached Frederick from Harrisburg: "Lee . . . concentrating all his forces . . . near Chambersburg."

9

Wednesday 1 July

GETTYSBURG, PENNSYLVANIA

Damp, clear dawn. From wet bivouacs and ditches, foot soldiers of 2 armies sleepily form ranks, hitch rifles and haversacks, and stiffly take up the march. Behind them creak gun teams and supply wagons. Some cavalry units have ridden all night.

Trudging heavy fields, skirmishers in open order head Heth's advance on Gettysburg. At 5.30 a.m., 1½ miles west of town, where the Chambersburg pike dips to cross the Willoughby Run, Federal outposts spot movement. Corporal Hodges rides forward, is fired on, fires back, and raises the alert.

Buford's Federal cavalry dismount to form a defensive line along the Run. Confederates grow in numbers; firing swells. By 8, all Heth's brigade is deployed. Buford runs up a gun battery, Confederate artillery replies.

Reynolds, 3 miles southward, hears the boom of gunfire and hastens ahead.

Back at Taneytown, telegram of Lee's concentration came in to Meade's H.Q. about 6. Meade draws provisional orders for army's withdrawal, if attacked, to a line along Pipe Creek. But Reynolds is already on the road to Gettysburg, where enemy were sighted, yesterday. Meade sends for his views: will the country there make a good base to fight on?

With battle possible, Federal army corps are dangerously spread over 25 miles: I and XI near Reynolds, III behind at Emmitsburg, XII west at Two Taverns; II near Meade; V and VI away east at Hanover and Manchester. Cavalry mainly further east still. Awaiting definite news, Meade orders spare wagons to the rear, and distant VI corps to be ready to move "at a moment's notice".

Meanwhile Reynolds reaches Buford. Telling him to hold on, he gallops back to lead up the Ist or "Iron" brigade of his first division. Buford's cavalrymen are forced back into woods. Reynolds's escort troops break down fences to open a short cut across fields and, fifes playing, the 2nd Wisconsin regiment marches into action.

Fighting spreads; Reynolds sends back a message: "Enemy advancing in strong force . . . I will fight them inch by inch . . ." He directs up more units, then falls shot through the head. "He never spoke a word, or moved", said his orderly.

11.15 a.m.: Meade's best general is dead. General Doubleday takes over from Reynolds. General Oliver Howard brings up his XI corps, takes over from Doubleday, and sends his troops through town to form new lines northwards.

Meade, about noon, gets messages in a rush. From Reynolds, from Buford, then the bombshell: Reynolds is "killed or badly wounded". At 1.10 p.m. he orders General Winfield Hancock up to Gettysburg to assume command; if he advises the ground there is good to

fight on, Meade "will order all the troops up".

gentlemen, we fight the decisive battle of the war."

Westwards, on the Cashtown road, Lee himself, forcing past his toiling columns, rides towards echoing gunfire. He comes on the field about 2 p.m., severely worried. No one has authorized battle; his army, like Meade's, is dispersed. Suddenly grey battle lines are seen to the north. Coming in by a fluke exactly on the Federal flank, 2 divisions of Ewell are marching back from original invasion. Howard's men break, begin to run.

Seizing the chance of sweeping victory, Lee orders Hill's corps to full attack. Inside an hour, despite a desperate stand by I corps, the Federals, caught in front and flank, are in rout. Units in fragments, bluecoats stream through the town. Droves are captured in narrow streets before survivors form shaky line in a hilltop cemetery. Hill has suffered heavy losses; Lee sends to Ewell: one good "push" should clear the hill.

Minutes, hours, pass, with no attack. Hancock reaches the cemetery after 5 p.m., organizing, inspiring, aligning Federal defences. General Henry Slocum arrives, ahead of his XII corps; III is approaching, II on the march. "I think we will be alright until night." Hancock sends to Meade at 5.25.

By 6 p.m. Meade senses withdrawal to new positions is no longer possible. VI corps is ordered to a forced night march; everyone is to make for Gettysburg. Meade is heard murmuring to his staff "Tomorrow,

In town, another message to Ewell bore no result. At dusk Lee rides across, to find Ewell utterly unnerved by the new responsibility of corps command in actual combat. Early does the talking, arguing that even with all 3 divisions of the corps now up, Union defences on Cemetery Hill are too strong to attack. Ewell seems helpless; Lee finally decides on a flank attack by Longstreet's 1st corps, now approaching, as soon after dawn as possible. Ewell's divisions will support, awaiting the sound of Longstreet's guns.

It is 10.20 p.m. before Meade's H.Q. advance party rides out from Taneytown, spurring their way through a "road blocked by troops and artillery moving to the front", taking "57 minutes by the watch" to cover 8 miles, writes Meade's son and aide, George. 15 minutes with General John Gibbon, temporary commander of II corps, then 3½ miles more.

At 11.45 Meade wearily dismounts by the cemetery gateway. Greetings over, gathered generals affirm the position is good. Meade remarks drily he is "glad to hear it . . ." As he stares, preoccupied, into the night, his brain races. Will Lee attack before daylight? How many men can be in position before he does? Has Lee gathered his whole force, or only part? Darkness yields no clue.

ARMY OF THE POTOMAC (FEDERAL or UNION) Approx. 90,000 men
Major-General George G. Meade commanding. His son, George, as Aide to Headquarters

I CORPS (Maj-General John Reynolds, then John Newton) with own Artillery Bde. (Wainwright)
    1st Division (Wadsworth) of 2 Bdes.
    2nd Division (Robinson) of 2 Bdes.
    3rd Division (Doubleday) of 3 Bdes.

II CORPS (Maj-General Winfield Hancock) with own Artillery Bde.
    1st Division (Caldwell) of 4 Bdes.
    2nd Division (Gibbon) of 3 Bdes. (Haskell as Aide to Gibbon; Goddard and Marvin, 1st Minnesota, in 1st Bde.)
    3rd Division (Hays) of 3 Bdes. (Allen, 14th Indiana, in 1st Bde.)

III CORPS (Maj-General Daniel Sickles) with own Artillery Bde. (Tremain as Aide to Sickles)
    1st Division (Birney) of 3 Bdes.
    2nd Division (Humphreys) of 3 Bdes. (Bardeen, 1st Massachusetts; Blake, 11th Massachusetts, in 1st Bde.)

V CORPS (Maj-General George Sykes) with own Artillery Bde.
    1st Division (Barnes) of 3 Bdes.
      (Colonel Sweitzer commanding, and Bancroft and Houghton, 4th Michigan, in 2nd Bde. Chamberlain, 20th Maine; Colonel Vincent, commanding, and Norton in 3rd Bde.)
    2nd Division (Ayres) of 3 Bdes. (Farley, 140th New York, in 3rd Bde.)
    3rd Division (Crawford) of 2 Bdes.

VI CORPS (Maj-General John Sedgwick) with own Artillery Bde.
    1st Division (Wright) of 3 Bdes.
    2nd Division (Howe) of 2 Bdes.
    3rd Division (Newton) of 3 Bdes.

XI CORPS (Maj-General Oliver Howard) with own Artillery Bde.
    1st Division (Barlow, then Ames) of 2 Bdes.
    2nd Division (Steinwehr) of 2 Bdes.
    3rd Division (Schurz) of 2 Bdes.

XII CORPS (Maj-General Henry Slocum) with own Artillery Bde.
    1st Division (Williams) of 3 Bdes. (Hutchinson, 3rd Maryland, in 1st Bde. Benton, 150th New York, in 2nd Bde.)
    2nd Division (Geary) of 3 Bdes. (Jones, 60th New York, in 3rd Bde.)

CAVALRY CORPS (Maj-General Alfred Pleasanton) with own Horse Artillery in 2 Bdes.
    1st Division (Buford) of 3 Bdes.
    2nd Division (Gregg) of 3 Bdes.
    3rd Division (Kilpatrick) of 2 Bdes.

ARTILLERY RESERVE (Tyler) of 5 Bdes. (Brig-General Henry Hunt commanding all Artillery.)

Chief of Engineers: Maj-General Gouverneur Warren.

SIGNAL CORPS Capt. Norton commanding.

NEWSPAPER CORRESPONDENTS ON BATTLEFIELD
Carpenter (*New York Herald*). Coffin. Crounze ("Bonaparte" in New York *World*). Reid ("Agate" in Cincinnati *Daily Gazette*). Wilkeson (*New York Times*).

BATTLE

ARMY OF NORTHERN VIRGINIA (CONFEDERATE) Approx. 70,000 men.

General Robert E. Lee commanding. Colonel Long on Headquarters' Staff.

I CORPS (Lieut-General James Longstreet)
    1st Division (McLaws) with Cabell's Bn. of Artillery
        Kershaw's Bde. (South Carolina)   Barksdale's Bde. (Mississippi)
        Semmes's Bde. (Georgia)   Wofford's Bde. (Georgia)
    2nd Division (Pickett) with Dearing's Bn. of Artillery
        Garnett's Bde. (Virginia)   Kemper's Bde. (Virginia)
            (Dooley, 1st Virginia, and Johnston, 7th Virginia)
        Armistead's Bde. (Virginia)
    3rd Division (Hood) with Henry's Bn. of Artillery
        Law's Bde. (Alabama)   Robertson's Bde. (Texas)
        (Colonel Oates, 15th Alabama,   (Bradfield, 1st Texas; Giles and West, 4th Texas;
          Colonel Perry, 44th Alabama)   Major Rogers, 5th Texas)
        Anderson's Bde. (Georgia)   Benning's Bde. (Georgia)
    Artillery Reserve (Walton) of 2 Bns. (Colonel Alexander commanding Alexander's Battalion)

II CORPS (Lieut-General Richard Ewell)
    1st Division (Early) with Jones's Bn. of Artillery
        Hays's Bde. (Louisiana)   Smith's Bde. (Virginia)
        Hoke's Bde. (North Carolina)   Gordon's Bde. (Georgia)
    2nd Division (Johnson) with Latimer's Bn. of Artillery
        Steuart's Bde. (Maryland,   Walker's Stonewall Bde. (Virginia)
          North Carolina, Virginia)
        (McKim as Aide to Bde. H.Q.)   Jones's Bde. (Virginia)
        Nicholls's Bde. (Louisiana)   (Boatwright, 44th Virginia)
    3rd Division (Rodes) with Carter's Bn. of Artillery
        Daniel's Bde. (North Carolina)   Doles's Bde. (Georgia)
        Iverson's Bde. (North Carolina)   Ramseur's Bde. (North Carolina)
    Artillery Reserve (Brown) of 2 Bns. (Robinson Berkeley in Nelson's Bn.)

III CORPS (Lieut-General Ambrose Hill)
    1st Division (Anderson) with Lane's Bn. of Artillery
        Wilcox's Bde. (Alabama)   Mahone's Bde. (Virginia)
        Wright's Bde. (Georgia)   Perry's Bde. (Florida)
        Posey's Bde. (Mississippi)
    2nd Division (Heth) with Garnett's Bn. of Artillery
        Pettigrew's Bde. (North Carolina)   Brockenbrough's Bde. (Virginia)
        Archer's Bde. (Alabama and Tennessee)   Davis's Bde. (Mississippi and North
                      Carolina)
    3rd Division (Pender) with Poague's Bn. of Artillery
        Perrin's Bde. (South Carolina)   Lane's Bde. (North Carolina)
        Thomas's Bde. (Georgia)   Scales's Bde. (North Carolina)
    Artillery Reserve (Walker) of 2 Bns.

CAVALRY CORPS Stuart's Division with Beckham's Bn. of Horse Artillery
        Hampton's Bde.   Robertson's Bde. (North Carolina)
        (North and South Carolina, Georgia)
        Fitz Lee's Bde. (Virginia)   Jenkins's Bde. (Virginia)
        Jones's Bde. (Virginia)   Lee's Bde. (North Carolina and Virginia)
    Imboden's Command (Virginia)

FOREIGN OBSERVERS WITH THE ARMY
Fremantle (Lieut-Colonel of Coldstream Guards, British Army)
Ross (British Captain of Hussars in Austrian Army)
Scheibert (Captain of Prussian Royal Engineers)

Field Limber

12 pounder Field Gun

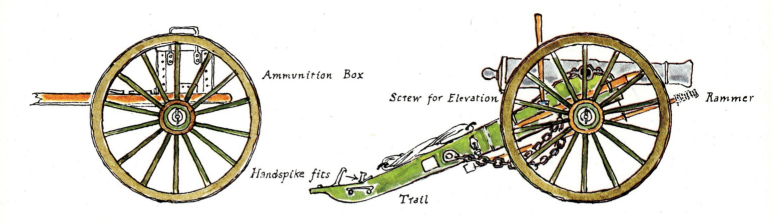

Ammunition Box

Screw for Elevation

Rammer

Handspike fits

Trail

Hammer to Detonating Cap

Adjustable Backsight

Foresight

Bayonet

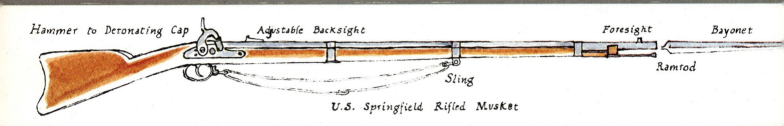

Sling

Ramrod

U.S. Springfield Rifled Musket

U.S. Telegraph Corps Wagon

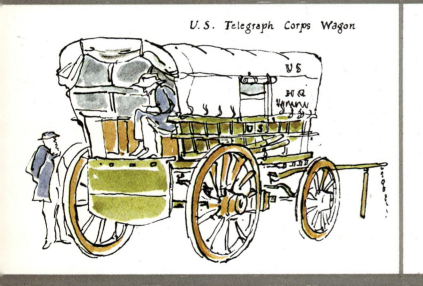

U.S. Ambulance

Trench

Cheval-de-Frise

Pontoon Bridge

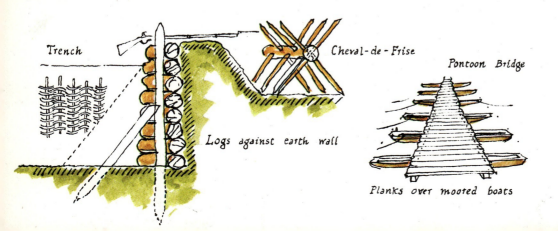

Logs against earth wall

Planks over moored boats

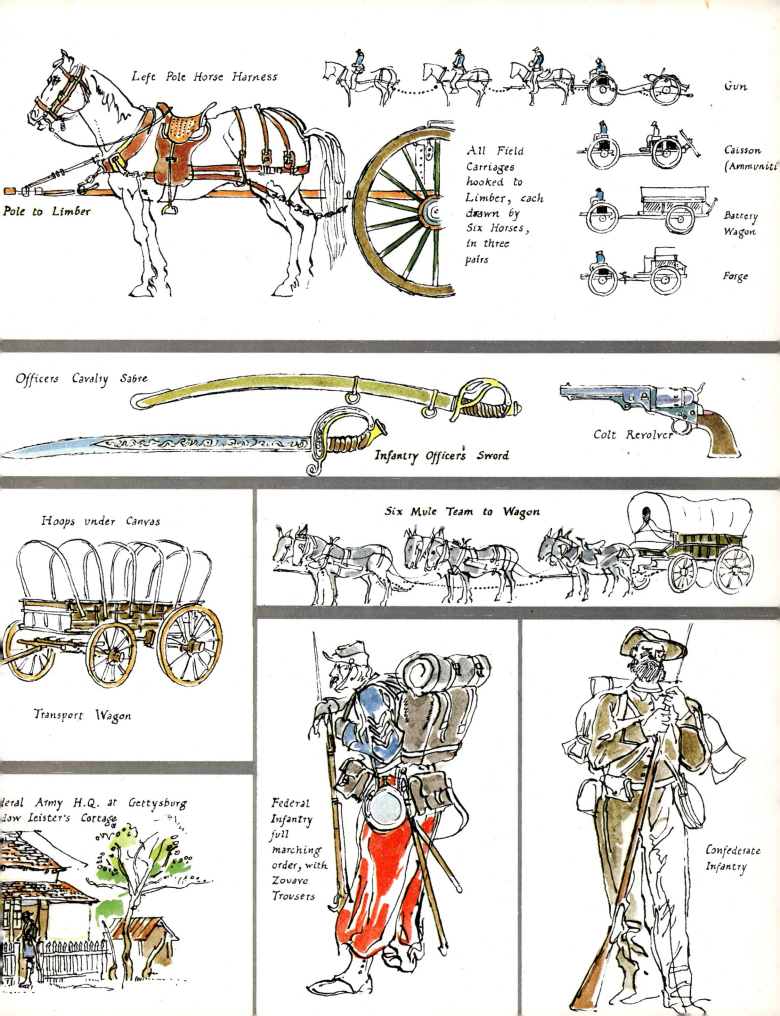

Left Pole Horse Harness

Pole to Limber

Gun

Caisson (Ammuniti

Battery Wagon

Forge

All Field Carriages hooked to Limber, each drawn by Six Horses, in three pairs

Officers Cavalry Sabre

Infantry Officers Sword

Colt Revolver

Hoops under Canvas

Transport Wagon

Six Mule Team to Wagon

Federal Army H.Q. at Gettysburg dow Leister's Cottage

Federal Infantry full marching order, with Zouave Trousers

Confederate Infantry

1 a.m. Thursday 2 July

GETTYSBURG, PENNSYLVANIA

Town shaken to its roots, citizens in cellars, many fled. In the main square smashed wagons, corpses. Streets "strewn over with clothes, blankets, knapsacks . . . dead horses . . ." writes a Lady of Gettysburg in her diary. Confederates foraging. "We watched the Rebels rob the house opposite . . . loading up . . . a large four-horse wagon." Hundreds of wounded, mostly Federals, fill churches and houses. General Barlow: "three confederate Surgeons . . . gave me chloroform and probed my wound . . . gave me some morphine".

CEMETERY HILL

General Henry Hunt, Federal Chief of Artillery, and staff officers guide Meade out beyond the Baltimore pike to gun batteries sited on the brow of the hill. Troops are sleeping in battle lines; invisible on lower slopes stand watching pickets; an occasional bullet whines. Northwest across the valley the faint glow of enemy camp fires. Fitful moonlight hides all but general features; Meade defers full inspection of the position until daylight.

Outcome of battle will be decided by 4 factors: each army's speed in concentration; each commander's choice of ground for attack and defence; available artillery; men's morale. Meade feels exposed, unready, insecure. Crack I corps is shattered, much of XI fled yesterday at first fire. XII is up and élite II near, but III, southward, he considers badly generalled; his own tough regulars of V are still on the Hanover road; VI, biggest of all, is more than a day's march away. And somewhere in the darkness lies all or part of the most famous fighting force of the war: unbeaten veterans, superbly confident, brilliantly led. Meade's orders to shield Washington preclude any risks; battle lost here could mean Lee in the capital dictating terms, the Union perhaps destroyed for ever.

Meade had not asked to command an army. Exactly 94 hours ago, 3 a.m. Sunday, an officer from Washington awoke him in his tent with President Lincoln's appointment. He took it with little joy "obeying this order . . . totally unexpected and unsolicited . . . I have no promises . . . to make", he announced in Orders.

48-year-old Regular, ex-railroad engineer and lighthouse designer, violent tempered, with baggy clothes and pouch-lined eyes, Meade shows little glamour to his men. With reading glasses over beaked nose he struck Reid as more "thoughtful student than . . . dashing soldier". But his reputation is growing. When

Lee heard of his appointment, he said: "Meade will commit no blunder in my front . . ."

South of town, Confederate infantry gradually taking position. General Hays: "About 2 o'clock . . . I moved my troops into an open field." Each man rolls himself in his thin blanket, rifle within reach. At least tonight is dry.

About 2 a.m. a horseman is brought under guard to Ewell; his captured message reveals Federal V corps only 4 miles away, at Bonaughtown. "I shall resume my march at 4 a.m.", General George Sykes has written. Ominous news, and addressed to XII corps; how many more Federals nearing Gettysburg?

CHAMBERSBURG, PENNSYLVANIA

24 miles away, across South Mountain, rearguard of Lee's army. "About 2 o'clock . . . aroused by the sound of the long roll, we were quickly in line", writes David Johnston, 7th Virginia Regiment. As General George Pickett's division breaks into a fast route step, the rest of Longstreet's corps stretches almost to Gettysburg. Near Greenwood gun teams of reserve artillery stand hitched, waiting for road space; ahead for miles General John Hood's division is tramping all night, drops for 2 hours' rest by the roadside. Confederates march light: rifle, rolled blanket, haversack, cartridge box, shoes if lucky. Yesterday whole corps halted 8 hours when lead division, under General Lafayette McLaws, jammed into a 14-mile-long wagon train with Ewell's rear division emerging from a side road, returning from the north. Marching again from 4 p.m. to midnight, McLaws's men are now bivouacked, advance brigade 2 miles from Gettysburg.

At 2.30 a.m. reserve artillery rumbles on to the road, at 3 General Evander Law's Alabaman brigade sets out from New Guilford.

ROUND TOP HILLS, SOUTH OF GETTYSBURG

Federal II corps, sleeping in battle lines across Taneytown road, hauled to its feet at 3 a.m. "We wer aroused . . . told to hurry & make coffe which we got half done & Orders to fall in" writes Sgt. Matthew Marvin, 1st Minnesota. Beyond the hills, head of III corps stumble through a maze of fenced farmland; one brigade strayed 3 miles north almost into enemy outposts. Capt. Tremain, guiding units in, half lost himself, sees dimly "a column of men . . . silently passing . . . Were they blues or greys?" before he recognizes friends.

Eastwards, 1st division of V corps, miles ahead of rest, camped along Baltimore pike, "frequently awakened by . . . other Troops coming in . . . ratling of canteens and the command of officers was herd all Night." *James Houghton's journal*. His regiment, 4th Michigan, fell out "to tired to cook . . . ate . . . raw pork hardtack and sun cooked coffee", but gets scant rest. "Up at 3.30 a.m. Inspect arms." writes his mate, John Bancroft. Numb fingers work ramrod and rag in rifle bores; weary officers check firing hammers and ammunition. 10 minutes later, lead division of XII corps ordered to press forward; "directed to drop knapsacks, tents and blankets . . ." writes Charles Benton.

Few veterans stagger under full 85 lb load of equipment; discarded clothing litters half Maryland. Two weeks' relentless marching has cost thousands of casualties from sunstroke, dysentery, exhaustion. In II corps alone "70 men who fell dead . . . about 1200 disabled . . ." wrote Charles Goddard 12 days ago.

Along clay roads in moonlight, men march as in a dream. Bands silent, joking died, ranks shuffle through gravel and dust. Wagons and gun carriages creak at intervals; cracking whips and sudden, high swearing from drivers; mostly silence. Down the spokes of a giant wheel, for scores of miles columns in blue and grey are converging on a central hub, a country town almost no one has heard of.

4.15 a.m. Thursday

GETTYSBURG, PENNSYLVANIA

30 minutes to dawn. In pallid half-light Lee finishes a hasty breakfast, probably eating little. 56 now, showing the strain of active service, he is "in the saddle before it was fairly light", writes Colonel Long. Riding up on a ridge, near the looming shape of a Lutheran Seminary, he joins General A. P. Hill's Corps H.Q., where "everything exhibited signs of preparation for action". Lee orders Capt. Johnston of Engineers to prospect the land lying south and eastwards, marking approach roads for troops and obstacles to an advance; and Colonel Long to help select and check gun-positions with a clear field of fire on to Cemetery Hill, just becoming visible opposite.

Lee has little now to do pending the arrival of Longstreet's corps, due very soon. Reporting last night his leading troops within 2 miles of town, Longstreet was told to prepare attack for as soon after daylight as possible. Cap badges of Federal prisoners yesterday were all of I and XI corps; Sykes's intercepted message means V, marching "at 4 a.m.", still 4 miles away; XII maybe up; but rest of Meade's army almost certainly not yet in position. Equally certain, it is gathering fast. A determined, sudden assault, launched at once before the whole Army of the Potomac outnumbers him, offers Lee the best chance of success.

Lee's manner of quiet confidence hides certain doubts. Ideally he would have preferred a mobile campaign to pitched battle; but, strategically, he has no choice. Slow retreat through the mountain passes would cramp his army along a narrow, vulnerable road; a move around Meade's flank towards Washington, such as Longstreet urged yesterday, would mean hauling miles of wagons blindly across an enemy flank with no cavalry to report just where the flank is. Word finally in from Stuart puts his errant squadrons miles north at Carlisle, useless.

Not only is Lee without cavalry but for the first time without the incomparable "Stonewall" Jackson. Two corps commanders are inexperienced, Ewell suddenly indecisive. Only senior general, bushy-browed "Bulldog" Longstreet, is dependable but, in Lee's unguarded words, "so slow".

The men themselves, however, Lee thinks invincible; and they worship "Uncle Robert". Religious, distressed at civil strife but loving Virginia, he wrote when resigning his U.S. commission: "Save in defence of my

native State, I never desire again to draw my sword." On Sunday he told a Chambersburg woman that "war was a cruel thing . . . he only desired that they would let him go home and eat his bread there in peace".

2 miles away, Meade has finished inspecting his lines. About ¾ mile south of the cemetery a farm cottage stands near the Taneytown road, midway down the whole Federal position on the crest. Meade marks the widow Leister's house as Army H.Q., and Capt. Norton begins setting up H.Q. signal station behind.

Meade anxiously questions General Hunt: III corps ammunition train is back at Emmitsburg, leaving only supplies in the caissons; I and XI fired heavily yesterday; will ammunition last out a full battle? Hunt confesses he has built up a secret reserve column carrying an extra 20 rounds "for every gun in the army . . . there would be enough . . . but none for idle cannonades".

Across fields behind the ridge 14 gun batteries of Artillery Reserve still drawing in. Telegraph train, with batteries on pack mules, waits at Taneytown, but hundreds of canvas-topped wagons laden with food and shell already glimmer in the greyness. Horses,

orderlies, teamsters, men lost, men swearing: an immense, sprawling supply park. And mules. Given strong language and steady whipping, mules will haul a wagon almost anywhere, eventually. Buried in the throng are 2 hospital wagons with tinned food, blankets, bandages, sent from Frederick by the Sanitary Commission in Washington. Mr. Hoag squeezed them in "just before the headquarters teams", but Major Bush has ridden ahead and "in the vast concourse I was unable to find them that night".

Some 5 miles west, the general detailed to direct Lee's main attack appears unhurried. "Breakfasted with General Longstreet and his staff", writes Capt. Ross, an observer from the Austrian Huzzars. Longstreet's leading troops "were up and ready to move at 4", reports General Joseph Kershaw, but road still blocked by Ewell's rearmost wagons. Back at Cashtown, Hood's Texans, after 2 hours rest, "awakened . . . within 10 minutes were on their way. . . . Falling into a swinging route step", writes J. B. Polley.

4.45 a.m. Thursday

GETTYSBURG, PENNSYLVANIA

Dawn. Sky clouded; sultry; ground mist. Lee, with a group of officers on the crest of Seminary Ridge, probably near Shultz's house, studies intently the hill opposite, some 1,500 yards away. Magnified by their fieldglasses, but still flat shapes against the sunrise, lines of the cemetery grow sharper minute by minute. Near the brick gateway barrels of cannon, behind low stone walls the glint of rifles. Figures moving.

Directly in front, Gettysburg Middle Street is deserted; to the right, where Baltimore Street branches below the cemetery, Snyder's Wagon Hotel silent. Beyond trees and belfries of the town, high forests. Closer, falling away diagonally to Lee's right, beyond the cemetery an open ridge; and, full 3 miles southwards, the faint silhouette of a rounded and densely wooded hill. Adjoining it a sister, rather lower, with clear lines as though bare of trees. In front of them woods, and a jagged pile of rock.

Millions of years before James Gettys laid out squares of a town, ancient sandstone of the region tilted westwards and split. Molten diabase rock forced upwards through the fissures to solidify into a sill running bandwise across country, south-east of the present town. Erosion left its western edge a harsh outcrop of blackish ironstone jutting from the rich soil, harder than granite, scaling sometimes into boulders and flakes, quarried mainly for tombstones and road chippings. Trees, shallow rooted, cling to the sides, thorn bushes and brambles sprout from jagged cracks in the rock face. In places walls rise sheer, almost unclimbable. Cemetery Hill, Culp's Hill, the round-topped hills to the south are parts of one formation.

Due south, Lee can see the Emmitsburg road glimmering ghostlike between its fences. 2 miles away it rises to a rural cross-roads by J. Want's peach orchard, then again to a crest by Snyder's house before it disappears beyond a belt of timber. The ridge he stands on runs also south, through woods and farms, towards the orchard. Between it and Cemetery Ridge opposite, an undulating valley of pasture and ripening corn-fields, studded with wooden farm houses, tapers towards the round-topped hills.

In a mobile campaign Gettysburg would have made a valuable base. No less than 11 roads converge on it; it has a railhead to Hanover and the east. Lee's troops control all western and northern roads and the town itself; yet in impending battle this means little. The core of the position is in Federal hands. On commanding slopes, with reinforcements certainly racing up, Meade holds a formidable strongpoint—but only half of it. In fast-growing light, Lee can make out no enemy whatever on the main ridge south. Immediate assault by Longstreet's corps on the crest, simultaneous with Ewell's attack from the town, must crush the cemetery

defences in a giant pincers.

But still no sign of even Longstreet's leading division. Every minute is vital. Should Ewell attack now, alone? Or perhaps retreat from his position to join with Longstreet in one massive blow later? A staff officer is sent at the gallop to ask Ewell's opinion.

CHAMBERSBURG PIKE

5 miles to the rear, Longstreet's H.Q. completing leisurely preparations. Colonel Fremantle, British observer from the Coldstream Guards, and an Austrian Army observer have been given horses to watch the battle. "The Austrian . . . had shaved his cheeks and cired his moustaches . . . as if he were on parade at Vienna," writes Fremantle.

TANEYTOWN

Still jammed by Federal H.Q. troops and supplies. Whole H.Q. staff, equipment in wagons, ready to move. At 5 a.m. Capt. Mendell ordered to march his engineer battalion to Westminster and Union Bridge to guard the lumbering supply trains "against any cavalry raid." Provost Marshall Patrick went forward 3 hours ago; a fenced compound, under guard, stands ready for prisoners. Chief of Staff Butterfield rides out at 5.30, leaving final message for Sedgwick, VI corps, to push on with all speed to Gettysburg.

SEMINARY RIDGE, GETTYSBURG

5.45 a.m. First of Longstreet's assault troops appear. Kershaw's brigade, able to march at sunrise, is pulling off the Chambersburg pike, behind the ridge. Rest of McLaws's division and Hood's close behind.

More arrivals at Lee's observation post: Hill, Heth, with a bandaged head-wound, all Longstreet's party, various staff officers. Ross: "We let our horses loose in an enclosed field . . . and lay . . . looking through our glasses at the Yankees." Capt. Scheibert, from the Prussian Army, says Fremantle has "never seen a fight before"; both are perched in the same tree, determined after crossing the Atlantic not to miss a detail. Below them Lee and his generals sit talking. Hood rides up, well ahead of his division, and is greeted by Lee: "The enemy is here, and if we do not whip him, he will whip us."

Longstreet thinks himself a strategist and has no shyness in pressing his views. Once again he has urged Lee not to attack but to move around the Federal flank towards Washington. Told plainly plans must stand, he is in a sour mood. He sits by Hood, where Fremantle can see them "whittling sticks". He growls: "The General

is a little nervous this morning; he wishes me to attack;
I do not wish to do so without Pickett. I never like to go
into battle with one boot off.''

But Pickett is a day's march away.

GETTYSBURG 2 July

ARMY OF NORTHERN VIRGINIA

Robert E. Lee commanding

Lee's **H.Q.**	early a.m			p.m.
I Corps	Longstreet			p.m
II Corps	Ewell	a.m.		p.m.
III Corps	Hill	a.m.		p.m

Longstreet's first approach march (Kershaw)

Longstreet's second march

Direction of Army's attack ⟶

ARMY OF THE POTOMAC

George G. Meade commanding

Meade's **H.Q.**	early a.m.		p.m		
I Corps	Newton	a.m.	p.m.	late p.m.	
II Corps	Hancock		p.m.	late p.m.	
III Corps	Sickles		p.m		
V Corps	Sykes		p.m.	late p.m.	
VI Corps	Sedgwick			late p.m.	
XI Corps	Howard	early a.m.	p.m	late p.m.	
XII Corps	Slocum	early am.	p.m	late p.m.	

Artillery Reserve and wagon trains

Sickles's Retreat ⟩⟩⟩⟩⟩⟩

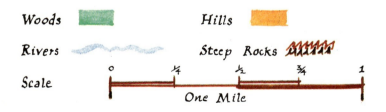

Woods		Hills
Rivers		Steep Rocks
Scale		

0   ¼   ½   ¾   1

One Mile

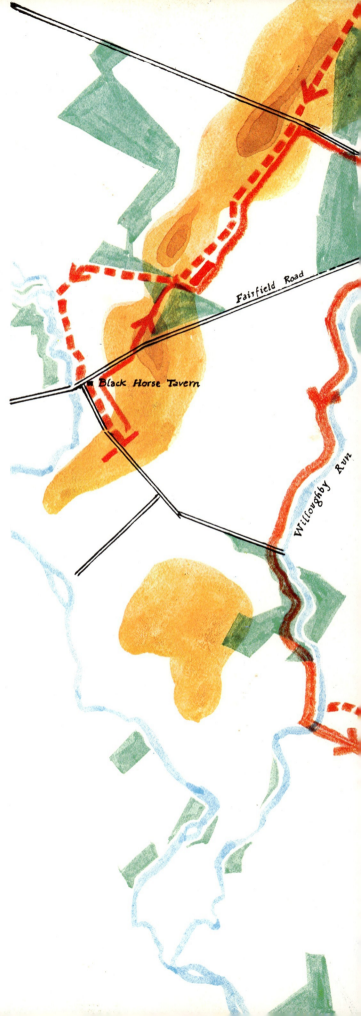

Fairfield Road

Black Horse Tavern

Willoughby Run

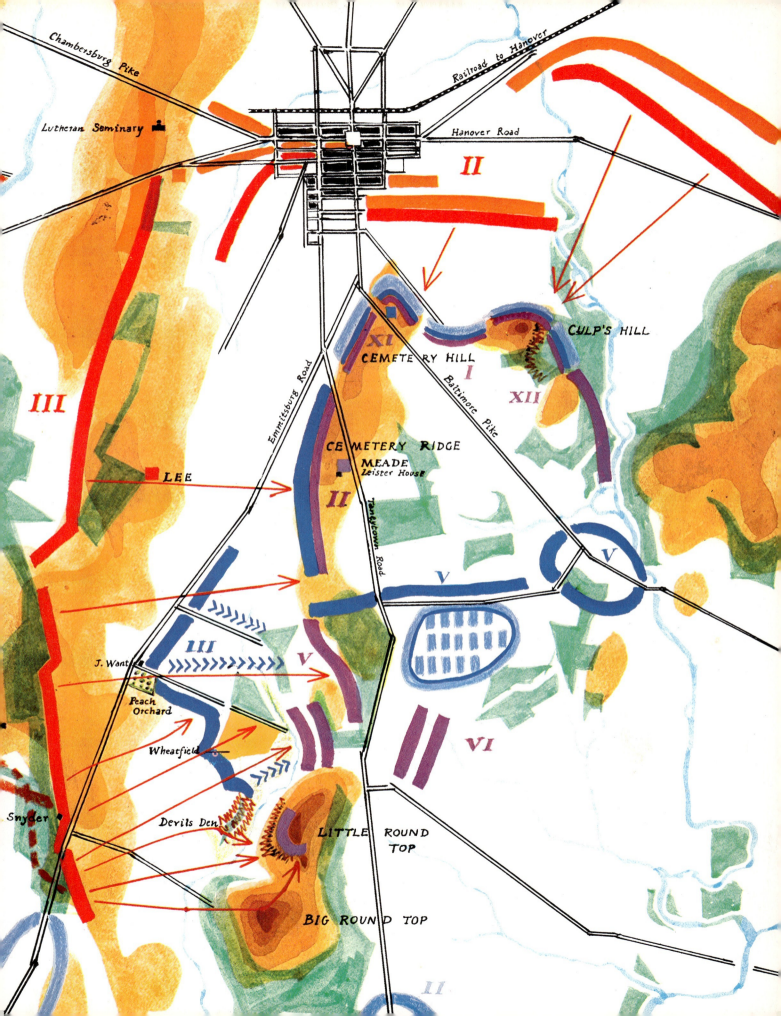

Chambersburg Pike

Lutheran Seminary

Railroad to Hanover

I

II

Hanover Road

CULP'S HILL

XI

CEMETERY HILL

I

XII

III

CEMETERY RIDGE

LEE

MEADE
Leister House

II

Emmitsburg Road

Baltimore Pike

Tanleytown Road

V

V

V

III

J. Want

V

VI

Peach
Orchard

Wheatfield

Snyder

Devils Den

LITTLE ROUND
TOP

BIG ROUND TOP

II

6 a.m. Thursday

PORT HUDSON, LOUISIANA

Main Confederate bastion on the lower Mississippi. An immense knoll, 2 miles across, with trenches zigzagging along high cliffs and siege guns commanding the river. Union army under General Banks investing from land and water, waiting to advance north. Baton Rouge, 12 miles south, already captured. 5th week of siege since direct assault failed murderously.

"We have dug ditches and . . . earthworks close to theirs, so close that our men and the 'Rebs' talk to each other, throw clods of dirt, and are up to all kinds of capers, it is the strangest warfare . . . one day the men will mutually agree not to fire . . . the next day every one who shows his head . . . is sure to be shot at," writes Capt. John Corden, 6th Michigan, to his wife on Saturday.

Local time 5 a.m. Offshore, U.S. cruisers *Hartford* and *Richmond* glisten in sub-tropic sunrise: this is the latitude of the Nile delta. Mortar batteries in gun-pits prepare for another day's unsupportable heat. Sickness rife; 6th Michigan numbers 160 men fit for duty. On the east bank Lt. Eaton moves out to a barn overlooking Confederate river emplacements. Watching Federal shellbursts on the cliffs, signalling back corrections to *Hartford* and thence by semaphore from masthead to mortars firing out of sight, he acts as observation officer for a crude directed fire—forerunner of later artillery practice.

In a hour he begins. His signal log, 6 a.m.:
Received. "Are you ready?" Later:
Received. "How was last shot from Howitzer?"
Sent. "touched the breastwork 8 ft to the right of the gun . . ."
Received. "And the last?"
Sent. "Had good range, but was 100 yds short."
Sent. "That burst short."
Sent. "Last shot was 100 yds to the right . . ."
Received. "It can't get any farther to the left. Where is the 2nd rebel gun?"

Signalmen constantly confuse numerals: 100 yds is read as 10, 75 as 45, 40 as 400. Not surprisingly, not one direct hit all day.

130 miles north, most vital Confederate city on the east bank of the Mississippi, key to whole Confederate west. Shattered houses, caves, earthworks, gun emplacements, cluster on one huge bluff, with cliffs sheer to the river. Inland, ravines and ridges, thick wooded, blocked by entanglements of chopped treetrunks. Beyond, smoke rises from a 15 mile circle of camp fires of a Union army. Today the 45th of total siege.

At Army H.Q. the general destined to become the Union's greatest commander, Ulysses S. Grant, probably already stirring. The campaign to cut central Mississippi has been a nightmare. First advance down Central Railroad lost supplies to raiders. After retreat and confusing orders, all Grant's army crossed the river to concentrate on the west bank above Vicksburg, but found the city's river batteries and Yazoo swamps to the north-east impassible. Through a raining winter soldiers slaved as navvies, digging canals, clearing bayous for boats, felling trees for log 'corduroy' roads over swamps. A final recrossing miles southward and 2 land battles drove a Confederate army helplessly into Vicksburg from the east. Direct attack failed, but on dry land at last, Grant's 3 army corps, some 35,000 men, have blocked all escape routes. A naval squadron patrols the river above and below.

After 6 weeks' gunfire still no surrender. Admiral David Porter says at Sevastopol "the great strongholds of the Malakoff town and the Redan . . . never in any way compared with the defense of Vicksburg". Chauncey Cooke, 25th Wisconsin, brought up by paddle steamer at night a week ago "lay on the hurricane deck . . . my head bolstered up on my knapsack . . . I watched the fire of our gun boats . . . down the river as broadside after broadside was poured into the city. . . . It seemed as if the shells from the mortars went up into the clouds a half mile. . . . They looked like meteors only their track was red."

Porter reports today "so hot . . . little can be done between 9 a.m. and 4 p.m. The mortars are kept going constantly night and day . . . am also placing 9, 10, and 100 pounder guns on scows".

Always enterprising, Porter led ships for weeks through narrowing channels to cut a route through the Yazoo jungle before they jammed and had to back: "animals of all kinds . . . coons, rats, mice, and wild cats were in the branches . . . sometimes a rude tree would throw Briarean arms around the smoke stack of the tin-clad *Forest Rose*, or . . . *Molly Miller*, and knock their bonnets sideways".

Ships move at daybreak. Capt. Woodworth: "got under way this morning with the *Benton*, *Mound City* and *General Price*, and went up abreast of 'Whistling Dick' battery and opened fire". Navy helps army. "General Herron signalled . . . he was out of ammunition for his 32-pounders . . . we could furnish him 200 rounds from the gunboats . . ." Some naval guns mounted ashore. Herron: "a battery of 42-pounder rifle guns . . . from the Navy . . . did excellent service . . ."

In trenches, usual dawn truce between opposing riflemen. "Little firing before the breakfast ration is eaten . . . sharpshooters . . . recline on the edges of the rifle pits . . . and keep up a running conversation," says tomorrow's *New York Herald*

Most men with pick and shovel, working in shifts against the heat, one hour on, one off. Traverses, saps, mines lengthen daily. Some galleries with timbered roofs reach 30 ft below ground. In front of XVII corps a 50 ft chasm breaching a Confederate strong point marks yesterday's mine exploded by 1,500 lbs of powder, "blowing some 7 or 8 rebels . . . engaged in countermining, within our lines," reports the corps engineer. One tough Negro survives.

Grant has decided on full assault on the 6th, if no surrender before. Approach saps are only feet from Confederate ditch. Today's orders: "heads of trenches . . . should be cut with gentle steps, so . . . troops can leave . . . rapidly . . ."

Lt. Haines, XIII corps engineer, has 2 barrels bound with vines to protect men digging the sap-head. On Tuesday a mirror raised on a pole revealed wheelbarrows working the enemy ditch; fearing countermining, he ordered a listening gallery dug. Yesterday fire bombs burned his sap roller, exposing the trench to rifle fire. He reports today: "I directed the head of the sap to be filled up tonight with sand-bags . . . only about 12 feet from the ditch."

Men are making "spring-boards" to lob shells over the parapet, others are boring out "mortars made of trunks of trees . . . said to work admirably for about 100 rounds . . ." To cross the ditch "grain sacks are being . . . filled with cotton . . . planks 18 ft long . . . prepared".

6 a.m. Thursday

GETTYSBURG, PENNSYLVANIA

Federal II corps goes into position on Cemetery Ridge. Lt. Frank Haskell, a Wisconsin lawyer now on 2nd division's staff, says: "The morning was thick and sultry . . . with low vapory clouds . . . all was astir upon the crests. . . . Men looked like giants there in the mist . . ."

Marvin: "we went to the right about 4 miles whare there was a new line forming Our Division [brigade] was the last reserve we stacked arms with Orders to remain near the stacks."

2 brigades from each division, 6 in all, deploy in line; each brigade covering a regimental frontage, with other 3 regiments to the rear as successive supports, 40 paces between regiments. 4 brigades in reserve.

Behind a screen of skirmishers, working parties out along the whole crest, tearing down rail fences which obstruct field of fire. In twos and threes other men are digging shallow trenches, coaxing damp wood, balancing billy cans over smoky fires for coffee. Fuel scrounged; wooden fence-rails vanish the moment an army, locust-like, bivouacs. Pillage actually forbidden; 1st Minnesota obeys strict orders. Marvin: "we wer not allowed to burn a rail & their was No wood so we pulled splinters & Bark off . . ."

Tuesday was pay-day for some units, but money is useless right now. Field kitchens and sutlers' wagons are with H.Q. teams at Westminster. Sutlers (civilian traders) are licensed robbers. Sgt. Allen, in line with 14th Indiana on II corps flank, wrote 5 weeks ago: "buter . . . at 60 cts per lb and eggs at 5 cts a peice and apples at 5 cts a peice . . ." In mid-campaign sutlers' stores are not the freshest, anyway. Capt. Castle: "Rancid sardines . . . sliced segments of ancient . . . cheese, with a top dressing of green fungus . . . engine-turned pickles, boiled in carbolic acid . . ."

If lucky, Federals carry haversack rations: 12 oz per day salt pork or 20 oz salt beef. $\frac{1}{10}$ lb green coffee or less roasted, 9 or 10 hard-tack biscuits. Tin dipper or cup to brew coffee in, tin plate as frying pan. Biscuits usually impossible to bite without soaking, sometimes mouldy. "When a man broke up his hard tack in his coffee, he might find the weevils swimming around on top." writes Bardeen, boy musician with III corps.

Some officers no better off. Colonel Wainwright,

commanding I corps artillery, last night had only "a cup of coffee and a hard-tack from some of the men, for none of our wagons were up . . ." This morning one of his batteries "without anything to eat today save what they could beg or borrow."

Westwards, on Seminary Ridge, a young Confederate with Ewell's reserve artillery awakes to find: "in a few feet of us . . . seventy-nine (79) North Carolinans laying dead . . . in a perfectly straight line . . . killed by one volley . . . I turned . . . sickened . . . and tried to eat my breakfast, but had to return it to my haversack untouched".

After 2 days' ride with 3 hours' sleep, correspondent Reid approaching Cemetery Hill "through crowds of slightly wounded, and past farm-houses converted into hospitals . . . up the slope of an exposed hill, and by the side of a smouldering camp-fire. . . . Batteries are all about us; troops . . . forming . . . Two or three general officers . . . come galloping by. Foremost . . . the Commanding General. He is not cheered, indeed is scarcely recognized".

ROCK CREEK VALLEY

S.E. of Cemetery Hill, advanced 2nd division of XII corps came in overnight; marches at 6.30 a.m. to extend Meade's defences to the right to Culp's Hill. Head of V corps, almost sleepwalking, has reached the bridge on the Baltimore pike. General Orders from Meade are read to the men: "commanders are authorised to order the instant death of any soldier who fails in his duty . . ." V corps is reserve. Colonel Joshua Chamberlain, 20th Maine: "Massed at first . . . on the right of the road . . . expecting every moment to be put into action . . ."

Benton, in XII corps: "As we neared the field . . . the first wounded man . . . passed us. His hand and arm were covered with blood . . . jesting ceased; a strange silence fell upon the marching columns . . ."

Surgeon Edwin Hutchinson, with XII corps on the Baltimore pike, writes his mother: "7 a.m. . . . the country people moving their families towards the rear. The women are all crying and children are screaming."

7 a.m. Thursday

LIVERPOOL, ENGLAND

Across the Atlantic, already noon on a fine day; "moderate S.S.E. wind" cutting the surface of the Mersey. Miles of docks form the main terminal for American and Canadian sea trade to Britain.

"O Johnny's gone to Liverpool,
  Away, you Heelo-o
To Liverpool, that Yankee school!
  John's gone to Hilo
Those Yankee sailors you'll see there
  Away, you Heelo-o
With red top-boots and short-cut hair
  John's gone to Hilo."

From the packed mass of shipping the plaintive cry of a shanty-man floats over the water. Sailors shout the chorus as they brace the yards of a merchantman, billowing canvas thundering above. Richer words are kept until out of earshot of land.

Merchant shipping still mainly sail. Loading in Princes Dock, for Lima, "The beautiful British-built clipper Barque *Eliza Hands* . . . 264 tons, AI at Lloyds"; for Valparaiso, the *Clarendon*, packet. Black Star line *Orient* "copper fastened . . . fast sailer" departed Monday. *Tonawanda*, monthly Philadelphia Line packet, sails in 10 days: "will take advantage of the steam tow-boats on the Delaware."

The Liverpool Mail lists more steamships every year. *Jura* sails today for Quebec. *Edinburgh* is off Ireland "calling at Queenstown to embark passengers and despatches" for New York: steerage fare, 5 gns, with food. Fabulous *Great Eastern* sailed Tuesday. Isambard Kingdom Brunel's dream ship has been unlucky from her launch. In 2 years time she will make money cable-laying; now she steams vast, half-empty, with "150 saloon passengers . . . 600 in the steerage . . . 300 . . . at Queenstown."

Despite civil war, immigration is booming. This year alone 146,813 make the Atlantic run to the U.S.A., packed on steerage decks like cattle.

Outside London on Woolwich Common, General Dacres, precisely at noon, is signalling the start of a mock battle and "great review" of garrison troops; otherwise England's capital is peaceful. Aristocracy at its country estates for the summer, many middle-class families already at the seaside. Donkey rides at Deal and Ramsgate, children with buckets, heavily clothed bathers swimming from machines wheel-deep in surf.

Out on Thames estuary, Gravesend has ships anchored from all over the world: *Henry Ellis* from New York, *Catherine Fernanda* from Genoa and scores of others arrived this morning.

Reaching across S.E. trade winds, somewhere in the Indian Ocean, 15 British clippers are racing with the new season's tea crop from China. *Fiery Cross*, 36 days out from Foochow, is in the lead, and will make London on 7 September after a run of only 104 days via Cape of Good Hope.

The Suez Canal has not yet shortened the eastern route for steamships; for years to come sailormen will be prey to long-shore sharks in all the ports of the world. Some ships have "class", some not. The New York girl who cleaned out the gullible Englishman in the song "Can't you dance the Polka?" spurns the "lime-juice sailor" at the end; her "regular" is of the élite: "My flash man he's a Yankee . . . And he sails in the Black Ball Line."

Near Liverpool, England, 2 secret ships are building in Laird's Birkenhead yard. Last July, James Bulloch, Confederate Secret Agent, commissioned 2 warships for the Confederacy. Although most British citizens— and certainly the cotton trade—still sympathise with the South, the British government is firmly pro-Federal. If the ironclads' ultimate destination were to become known officially, Britain could hardly let war material steam openly from a British port to aid "rebellion".

Thomas Dudley, U.S. Consul, has smelt a rat, already has spies in the yards. Bulloch does his best. He has told Laird's that the Confederacy, realising it would never get possession, has sold the ships, half completed, to the Pasha of Egypt. Bravay & Co are supposed to be French agents for the deal; Bulloch sits behind their desk in Paris, directing operations from a distance, and will "sell" the warships back to the Confederacy once they are safely clear of British territorial waters.

But they will never sail. Dudley's protests will lead to their seizure in October.

7 a.m. Thursday

SEMINARY RIDGE, GETTYSBURG

Lee walks alone under some trees. From time to time he watches the blue lines steadily extending opposite. Speed of enemy reinforcements changes everything; direct assault, uphill, will now mean heavy casualties. Still no sign of Longstreet's troops deployed, although all McLaws's division reported to have reached Herr's Tavern cross-roads a mile back.

Studying the ground closely, Lee devises yet another plan. If Longstreet's lines can form far enough southwards to overreach the Federal left, they could roll up Meade's flank; and if Longstreet's own left, sweeping up the Emmitsburg road, could seize and plant guns on the high ground by Want's peach orchard, Confederate gun-fire could blast Meade's artillery on Cemetery Hill. Ewell and Hill could then join a general assault, attacking from north and west.

Behind Seminary ridge more troops begin filing off the Chambersburg road into assembly areas beyond Willoughby Run. McLaws's leading brigade almost 1½ miles southward "halted at the end of the lane leading to the Black Horse Tavern," reports Kershaw. Hood's division mostly up but bunched along the main road. Colonel Alexander's battalion of reserve artillery "about 7 a.m. . . . halted in an grassy open grove . . . fed and watered."

By 7.30 Lee has decided his change of plan and given orders to Longstreet and Hill. McLaws, summoned to H.Q., finds Lee "sitting on a fallen tree with a map beside him." Lee points down the ridge and pencils a line on the map at right-angles to the Emmitsburg road. "I wish you to place your division across this road, and . . . to get there . . . without being seen by the enemy. . . . Can you do it?" McLaws can see no difficulty, saying he will ride ahead with skirmishers to explore a route; Lee suggests he goes with Capt. Johnston, already ordered to a reconnaisance.

Longstreet comes up in suppressed rage. Overhearing McLaws, he snaps: "No Sir, I do not wish you to leave your division." Longstreet points out on his own map a position not across but parallel with the road. Lee interrupts quietly: "No, General, I wish it placed just the opposite." Longstreet makes no reply but, when McLaws asks again to reconnoitre, sharply orders him back to his command.

Lee may not have heard all, but enough to realise things are seriously amiss. Plans changed and re-changed, dependent on accurate timing between army corps miles apart; delays; finally barely disguised antagonism from his senior general: poor auguries for success. Short of putting Longstreet under arrest, however, Lee can only rely on battle itself dissolving his subordinate's strange mood.

Longstreet at least begins preparations. He sends for

Alexander, best gunner in the army, and by-passing Colonel Walton orders him to direct the whole corps artillery in the attack.

At 8 a.m. infantry still resting, stretched on the ground, Kershaw, furthest south, can see 3 miles across the valley to where the Emmitsburg road rises clear of woods: "A large body of troops, with flankers out . . . passed . . ." Last 2 brigades of Federal III corps are joining main army.

CEMETERY RIDGE

Meade's position taking final shape. Inspection finished after daybreak, he drew approximate corps areas on Capt. Paine's sketch map; at army H.Q. engineers are tracing copies; staff officers sent to guide units into place. Army is strung out like a fish-hook. Northwards along the crest from the Round Tops, III corps links with II, and II with XI at Cemetery Hill; angled sharply east, I corps runs to Culp's Hill, XII south again to Baltimore pike; V in reserve. Only VI corps, and one division of V, still to come up.

Soldiers are digging rifle pits, piling rocks against walls to make breastworks, shielding cannon. On the slopes of Culp's Hill, General Greene's brigade holds the extreme left of XII corps. 60th New York are mainly farmers and woodsmen. Capt. Jones: "men felled the trees, and blocked them up into a close log fence. Piles of cordwood . . . set slanting on end against the outer face . . . made excellent battening . . . regiments, which had spades and picks, strengthened their work with earth." Trenches are dug, boulders set, rifle loopholes roofed with "head-logs", traverses cut. Within 2 hours the N.E. face of the hill will be a vast blockhouse.

Holding the cemetery, XI corps left dangerously thin after yesterday's fighting. General Schurz reports at 8 a.m., 3rd division lining the wall, "the whole . . . about 1,500 men." 1st division is down to "1,150 muskets".

Schurz: "about 8 o'clock . . . Meade quietly appeared . . . on horseback . . . His long-bearded, haggard face . . . looked careworn . . . I asked him how many men he had on the ground. . . . 'In the course of the day . . . about 95,000—enough, I guess, for this business.'

"And then . . . as if repeating something to himself: 'Well, we may fight it out here just as well as anywhere else.'

"Then he quietly rode away."

8 a.m. Thursday

Confederate capital has lived close to siege, more or less, since war began. Little outward change; maple trees and porticoes shade gracious streets; at the foot of a steep slope the James river gleams.

With Lee's army distant, city defences dangerously thin. *Daily Dispatch* today carries muster notices for volunteers: "HENRICO MILITIA . . . enrollment and drill . . . at 4½ o'clock P.M. in front of old Ashbury Chapel, Union Hill." 4th company of 179th Virginia Militia called, and "All French and Italian residents . . . to meet . . ." The mayor calls for "fifty mounted men" as guards.

Today a full alert: 25,000 enemy reported advancing from the east. The War Department, old Mechanic's Institute by 9th and Franklin, echoes strangely this morning to tramping feet. Head of Bureau of War, Robert Kean, his diary: "all the clerks and government employees, some 2,000 . . . ordered out under arms to the outer line of earth works . . . went out on the Darbytown road, some 8 miles. I went with them as a private . . ."

General Gorgas rides out today to inspect defences: "inner line . . . of considerable strength . . . ¾ to 1 mile farther from the city, is a continous line of rifle pits . . ."

16 miles east, danger to Richmond proves over-rated, only a "demonstration" by one Federal division to divert attention from a wrecking raid along the Pamunkey bridges northwestwards. And General Keyes is hardly Attila.

Constant prodding from H.Q. has failed to shift him; night sounds of enemy movement conjured too many terrors. 1½ hours ago he signalled: "moved back here . . . never seen a country so intersected with roads and swamps . . ." Staff officer John Gray writes tomorrow: "General Keyes . . . went 5 miles, got frightened, fell back . . . as worthless an old humbug as any the war has produced."

15 miles north, Pamunkey river soon under flames and smoke. Colonel Spear, 11th Pennsylvania Cavalry: "destroying 5 ferry boats . . . bridge at Widow Nelson's . . . burned to the water's edge".

Colonel Hall, with few Confederates at Hanover Junction, fears for vital Virginia Central Railroad linking the capital northwards. Hall to Richmond H.Q.: "collected about ½ of my force at the railroad bridge over North Anna, and will fight them there".

Any Union advance leaves more and more farms and houses destroyed, accidentally, wantonly, or as reprisals for suspected guerrilla sniping. In Ashland hospital, wild with rumours, one soldier bursts out today: "when I think of my wife and children homeless . . . I could set all Yankeedom in a blaze!" *Lady of Virginia's diary*

RICHMOND, VIRGINIA

James Seddon, Secretary of War, to Hall today: "I have sent you up 600 men, drawn from convalescents..."

2 years of war have drained all reserves of manpower. Kean's diary, when back at War Bureau, 12 July: "The conscription up to 40 is almost exhausted. Between 40 and 45 it will not yield probably over 50,000 men..." *Daily Dispatch* today: "WANTED *Fifty good size* BOYS, at the Government Bullet Factory on 7th..."

Crisis encourages slaves to desert. Mr. Greenhow advertises today: "$300 Reward Ran away, on the 25th inst., my man WILLIAM ... ginger bread colour ... also 2 boys "EDMOND & GEORGE left my house ..." But advancing Federal armies carry little spare food. Many slaves, escaping to "freedom" under the Union flag, simply find themselves herded in concentration camps, protected but almost starving.

Old U.S. Customs House on Main Street houses President's office and Cabinet room. "The President is ill today, and his physician is seriously alarmed ..." *Gorgas's diary*. Jefferson Davis never stops; all departments report to him; all war moves under his control. Strangely, revolutionary Richmond is more strangled by red tape than Washington. George Eggleston remembers "for a commissary general a crotchety doctor, some ... believed him insane." Soldiers passing Richmond wait hours for papers stamped; passport officials "daintily dressed, sat behind their railing, chatting and laughing" before opening office, while queuing soldiers missed trains to the front.

Upstream from city centre, thousands of Federal prisoners lie in tattered tents, hungry, on a sandy, treeless 6 acres on Belle Isle. Daniel McMann, captured today at Gettysburg, testifies later: "I saw a man kill a dog and eat part ... he sold the rest of it; I got some."

Hopeful excitement today; *Daily Dispatch* reports 940 prisoners embarking for the truce ship *New York* in Hampton Roads in exchange for 800 Confederates landed on Tuesday. Later today 49 more Union soldiers are marched from Broad Street rail depot down towards the docks, and pass under the painted sign *Libby & Son, Ship Chandlers and Grocers* to a warehouse prison. 50,000 men will have known its grimy walls before the end of the war.

A towering latticed bridge spanning the James river thunders to all trains rolling south. Through oak forests, pine woods, swamps, through fields of rice and cotton, 400 miles to Charleston, South Carolina. Visitors like the Prussian von Borcke last year are ravished by its villas, "its luxuriant gardens ... its sparkling sea-front, against which the blue wave broke gently ..." 3 miles across the harbour rises Fort Sumter where the whole war began.

The vital seaport has long beckoned northern strategists, dreaming of seaborne invasion. U.S. monitors sailed close 3 months ago, unleashed monster 15-inch guns, but retired battered before a hail of shore fire. Damaged harbour batteries and forts now repaired, Confederate gunners confident.

Beyond Sumter glint the flats of Morris Island, dugouts and emplacements of Battery Wagner barely visible. In 8 days' time its dunes will be churned to dust-clouds, entrenched, shelled, fought over with bitter savagery lasting a month, before Federals clear the island, land guns and shell Charleston.

OFF CAPE HATTERAS, N. CAROLINA

Fast steamer *Dinsmore*, 2 days out from New York, is exactly mid-passage to Port Royal. It brings Naval Ordnance Chief, Admiral Dahlgren, designer of new heavy guns, to command the Atlantic Federal blockading squadron in coming attack on Charleston.

8.30 a.m. Thursday

SEMINARY RIDGE, GETTYSBURG

Mist thinning, promise of heat. Colonel Long, in the saddle since 4, has ridden the length of the Confederate lines from N.E. to S.W., checking gun positions and reserve ammunition trains, preparing for the coming bombardment. The lull drags on with no sign of attack. Officers are wondering; Army of Northern Virginia usually hits fast.

Lee left the ridge about 8 to ride across to town to check with Ewell. Ewell was out on reconnaissance. Impatient to see the latest situation, Lee has been shown to the cupola of the county alms house. In full view, Federal defences are steadily strengthening on Cemetery and Culp's Hills. Lee rides quickly back to find Ewell. Later, "about 9 a.m." Long comes up to report. He says Lee "had been waiting there . . . expecting at every moment to hear the opening of the attack on the right, and by no means satisfied with the delay."

A mile south, correspondent Carleton Coffin has climbed the top of the cemetery gateway. Northward, he sees "newly mown fields . . . batteries with breast-works . . . cannoneers . . . besides their pieces . . . a beautiful farming country . . ." Eagerly noting every detail he rides "forward towards the town . . . Soldiers in blue were lying behind the garden fences . . . said one . . . 'The Rebels are right over there in that brick house.' . . .

"Ping!—and there was the sharp ring of a bullet over our heads."

$\frac{1}{2}$ mile south again, Meade emerges from Leister house H.Q. With most divisions up and digging in on chosen ground, his first worries are over. "He seemed in excellent spirits," writes his son George, who is told to ride to General Daniel Sickles, III corps commander, to ask if his lines are complete.

S.W. again, on the crest, Haskell is with II corps. At last signs of the enemy, as Hill's corps takes position opposite. Haskell: "About 9 o'clock . . . our glasses began to reveal them at the West and North-West of the town, a mile and a half away . . . They were moving towards our left, but the woods of Seminary Ridge so concealed them that we could not make out much . . ."

In the hazy distance behind the ridge, Capt. Johnston has returned from reconnaissance and been told to guide Longstreet's approach march: "Joined the head of Longstreet's corps about 9 a.m. . . . ." Hood's division still near the Chambersburg road, ordered to await Law's brigade, now only 6 miles away on forced march. Longstreet himself makes no move.

LOWER CEMETERY RIDGE

By 9.15 Meade's son George, clattering down the Taneytown road, has found the diamond flag of III corps floating among woods by Paterson's house. H.Q. is strangely silent. "No one but Capt. Randall . . . seemed to be about." George is told that Sickles had "been up all night" and "was resting in his tent". Randolph consults his chief, returns to say the corps is not in position because Sickles has had no instructions where to put it. George says he will find out and starts back up the road at the gallop.

9.30 a.m. Meade dictates orders to Slocum, XII corps, to prepare to attack once VI corps comes in:

"examine the ground in your front, and give . . . your opinion . . ." George arrives with the extraordinary news of Sickles. Meade considers Sickles has had his orders, tells George sharply to ride back and repeat that III corps is to prolong the line of II leftwards, connecting with it, and get "in position as quickly as possible."

North of town, Lee, again warning Ewell to be ready to move the moment he hears Longstreet's guns, has ridden off with Long to inspect the west face of Cemetery Ridge. Binoculars show troops and guns extending continually southwards. Every minute weakens Confederate chances. Lee feels his control slipping. "What *can* detain Longstreet?" he exclaims.

A gun battery on the slopes of Seminary Ridge turns out to be from Hill's corps, but Colonel Walker offers to guide Lee to where he thinks Longstreet is. He says Lee "manifested more impatience than I ever saw him show . . ." Overtaking some infantry marching south, "he even, for a little while, placed himself at the head of one of the brigades to hurry the column forward . . ."

10 a.m. Thursday

WASHINGTON D.C.

An open barouche is carrying the U.S. President's wife towards the White House. "Mrs. Lincoln . . . about 10 o'clock . . . was passing across the lot near the hospital . . ." *Washington Chronicle*. A snap, driver and seat are thrown off, horses bolt, Mrs. Lincoln leaps clear and falls headlong, stunned. Surgeons run up; at the hospital they find "no bones were broken".

Beyond its grand public buildings, Washington a sprawling village, transformed by war. Dusty avenues noisy with soldiers; bar-rooms full; carts, carriages, harness sparkling under the trees. "always on the go . . . trains of army wagons . . . sometimes they will stream along all day . . . great camps . . . in every direction . . . wagons, teamsters . . . the 47th Brooklyn . . . reg't is on the Heights," writes Walt Whitman next Tuesday. Tomorrow, "for more than an hour, again long strings of cavalry, several regiments . . . coming in town from north. Several hundred extra horses, some of the mares with colts, trotting along." The next evening Whitman "watching a cavalry company . . . making their night's camp . . . opposite my window . . . fires already blazing . . . men are driving in tent poles, wielding their axes . . ."

War Office now knows Lee is 70 miles away. General-in-Chief Halleck today orders Capt. Mears, at Relay House: "Move across the front of the Washington fortifications, scouting the country, and reporting . . . any . . . enemy."

In the telegraph rooms, operators tapping, instruments clicking. Hour by hour this week yellow paper copies of cypher telegrams relate the crisis. "went . . . to War Department. The President was there, and we read dispatches . . . from General Meade." *Navy Secretary Gideon Welles's diary*, today.

Just 9 years since Samuel Morse sent his first message, Annapolis Junction to Baltimore; in last financial year alone, 1,200,00 telegrams over military lines.

Lincoln has lived more in the telegraph rooms than in the White House this week. He rode in from summer lodgings at the hill-top Soldiers' Home this morning at 7. Boy in the Indiana backwoods, lumberman, store-clerk, postmaster, lawyer, reluctant politician, finally President inaugurated to face secession of the southern states, his life has never been easy. 54 now, his craggy figure and gaunt face look old.

Whitman, from his third storey lodgings in L street, often sees him rise past towards his office. 30 Cavalry guards have sabres drawn, but Lincoln's "equipage is rather shabby . . . horses indeed almost what . . . Broadway drivers would call *old plugs*. The President . . . in plain black clothes, cylinder hat," wrote Whitman 2 days ago. Lincoln looked to him "more careworn even than usual—his face with deep cut lines, seams, & his *complexion gray*, though very dark skin . . . very sad."

Whitman, one of America's greatest poets, stopped in Washington last January, returning from his wounded brother; he has stayed on as unpaid nurse to the hospitals. He has seen, first hand, the results of war. Last May the wounded "coming up in one long bloody string from Chancellorsville and Fredericksburg battles, six or seven hundred every day without intermission . . ." Writing 2 days ago: "Armory Square . . . contains by far the worst cases, most repulsive wounds . . . I go every day without fail, & often at night." Bringing small gifts, writing letters, giving men a will to live,

he makes every soldier his brother. Pocket books note mens' needs: "+Bed 15—wants an orange;" entries crossed when fulfilled. On Saturday he takes "several bottles of blackberry and cherry syrup, good and strong . . . Went through . . . the wards . . . gave them all a good drink . . . with ice water . . . prepared it all myself, and served it around".

Often lonely death. One Wisconsin lieutenant this summer: "water pail by . . . the bed, with . . . blood and bloody pieces of muslin, nearly full . . . his great dark eyes with a glaze already upon them . . ."

BALTIMORE, MARYLAND

In Mount Clare, vast workshops for Baltimore and Ohio Railroad, engineers hammering and riveting non-stop. With miles of track torn up by Confederate raiders, Washington ordered 5 iron-clad box cars armoured with steel rails. President Garrett was told "between 3 and 4 o'clock last Sunday . . ." Immediately rounding up workmen "many . . . at church . . . 300 have worked . . . day and night . . .", Garrett reports 2nd car completed this morning, rest by tomorrow.

A city violently divided; most citizens side openly with the South: 2 years ago Federal troops stoned in the streets. Union people keep to Eutaw House hotel; Barnum's and Maltby House reserved for "Confederates." Almost impossible to buy the true-blue *Tribune*; one correspondent told by a news-vendor "with a slight elevation of her nose . . . that she *never* took it".

Martial law proclaimed. Barricades closed by night; no-one can pass in or out except by giving military countersign. Bars and saloons closed at 8 p.m. Still expecting attack, volunteers flocking to defences, "already enrolled . . . over 10,000 Union Leaguers . . ." *New York Herald*

Passengers at Washington Branch Rail depot in confusion; trains running to Baltimore and north, but Northern Central branch to Harrisburg is cut, severing usual connections with Pittsburgh and "all points of the West". On one track, freight car 816 loading fast with medical supplies for Westminster, thence to Gettysburg.

10.30 a.m. Thursday

GETTYSBURG, PENNSYLVANIA

Confederate troops completing a northwestern arc facing the Cemetery. Union H.Q. signal station reported an hour ago: "enemy are moving . . . 5 regiments . . . to our right, accompanied by 1 four-gun battery . . ." 10.30 a.m. Slocum reports increased enemy strength on his flank, east of town, makes attack too risky.

Main Federal cavalry, exhausted, many "dismounted . . . , whose horses had fallen dead, . . . carrying their bridles . . ." approaching on Hanover road. At 10.40 patrols ordered against possible further enemy advance on Gettysburg from N.E. Lee's cavalry under Stuart on its last lap from Carlisle: "whole columns went to sleep in the saddle" during all-night march, writes John Cooke.

In town, from his observatory on Washington Street corner, Dr. Jacobs, Maths professor at Pennsylvania College, watches Rebel barricades going up. Federal marksmen from Cemetery Hill, sweeping the length of Washington and Baltimore Streets northwards, have made them a no-man's-land. Now, right through Gettysburg east to west, Ewell's troops are strengthening the south side of Middle Street with wood and earth. "they also broke down the fences on the northern side . . . to enable them to bring up reinforcements . . ." writes Jacobs. An occasional shot from Wainwright's artillery, ranging and fixing likely targets, explodes north of town. Otherwise only snipers' bullets break the silence.

11 a.m. Alexander, of Longstreet's artillery, since 8 a.m. exploring the woods along Seminary Ridge as far as Snyder's farm, 3 miles south, marking gun positions and fields of fire. "in about 3 hours had a good idea of all the ground, and had Cabell's, Henry's and my own battalions parked near . . ."

McLaws's infantry still north of Fairfield road beyond Willoughby Run. With it, Longstreet. About 11 a.m., Lee finally tracks him down. Longstreet explains surlily he is waiting for Law's brigade to come in. Lee, angry himself, gives an unusually categoric order: to move into position right now with what troops are up. Lee then rides south, fords the run and climbs the lane behind Pitzer's towards the right of Hill's corps, to a central viewpoint from which to watch the attack.

On the ridge opposite, George Meade has shuttled between Leister House and III corps H.Q. four times. An hour ago he found Sickles's "tents about to be struck, the general just mounted . . ." Sickles replied to Meade's message that "his troops were then moving . . ."

Back now at army H.Q., George sees Sickles arrive himself. Dan Sickles, bombastic politician who raised a volunteer regiment on credit, notorious for pistolling his wife's lover, is not Meade's favourite general.

George hears him complaining: his allotted ground is low for defence, useless for artillery. Meade, spectacles glinting, asks why, if part of XII corps held it last night, Sickles can't hold it now. Sickles retorts that Geary's troops simply bivouacked. There seems good high ground in front; cannot a staff officer help him site his artillery, and cannot he use his own judgement for his infantry?

Meade, preoccupied, is vague. So long as Sickles links the Round Tops with II corps, "any ground within those limits . . . I leave to you." Meade sends Hunt to help with Sickles's guns, and turns to other problems.

At 11 a.m. Slocum's advice against attack comes in. Meade finally decides on defensive battle. When the storm breaks, units will need to march swiftly to threatened points. To know all brigades' positions, staff officers attached to each corps are ordered to map-trace "positions of . . . artillery, infantry, and trains."

Reid, with note-pad, is allowed inside the crowded Leister cottage: "the Adjutant-Generals were . . . sending out the orders; aides and orderlies were galloping off . . . General Warren . . . with the General Commanding, poring over the maps . . ."

"Before 11 a.m. every desirable point of observation was occupied by a signal officer," reports Capt. Norton. On Cemetery, Culp's, Power's Hills, and, dominating all, on Little Round Top, red and black squared semaphore flags inter-connect every corps of the army.

Soon after climbing Round Top, earlier, Norton signalled: "Saw . . . infantry move into woods on ridge . . . See wagons moving up and down the Chambersburg pike . . . Think the enemy occupies the range of hills 3 miles W. of town . . ."

11 a.m. Thursday

NEW YORK CITY

Three midgets, around 32 inches high, march onstage in the lecture room of Barnum's "Grand Old Museum of Wonders" to enthusiastic applause. First act, commencing now, shows General Tom Thumb and wife Lavinia resplendent in wedding costumes; next echoes to drum of "redoubtable Commodore Nutt" while Tom impersonates Napoleon. The "ELPHIN MORTALS . . . no larger than so many babies . . . WHO CAN WONDER THAT CROWDS throng their levees every day?" advertises *New York Daily Tribune*.

Lincoln himself bent double to greet them at their wedding presentation last February.

A great commercial metropolis. Macy's, on 6th Avenue, advertises today: "Lace Goods, Embroideries . . . Shawls, Lace Mantillas, . . . Yankee notions, ribbons . . . N.B. we continue to sell our ladies' and gents' kid gloves at $1 a pair."

Streets mostly of dirt, unmade Board of Aldermen meets in 2 hours' time, votes that 58 and 63-65 streets, between 3rd and 5th Avenues "be graded and curb and gutter set." Vacant land bordering 3rd Avenue to be fenced in, part of 11th to be cobbled. "Dennis Ryer allowed to put watering trough on . . . corner of Broadway and 42nd Street." *Tribune*

Horses everywhere. "FOR SALE A pair of fine grey mares . . . very stylish drivers and fast . . . Call at . . . 28 Broadway, upstairs . . ." *Herald*

For "clergymen . . . and persons of literary habits" who need gingering up, "PLANTATION BITTERS" . . . Cascarilla bark, dandelion, wintergreen, snake root, burdock— among other ingredients. Cincinnati Soldiers' Home has dosed "hundreds of our noble soldiers . . . the effect is marvellous . . ." *Tribune*

For the mentally worried, Miss Wellington "the renowned English Prophetess" fortells "lawsuits, journeys . . . hidden treasures, enemies . . . Brave soldiers, learn your doom of glory, life or death . . . do not delay to visit . . . 101 Sixth Avenue . . ." *Herald*

Smoke settling in railway stations. Morning expresses for Albany, Buffalo, Philadelphia, Washington all departed. Passengers boarding the 11.30 slow for New Haven in the station on 27th street. Last freight loading at Pier 26, East River: *Bridgeport* steams in 1 hour. Port of New York the busiest in America; high water $1\frac{3}{4}$ hours ago. 9 steamers and 41 sailing vessels come in today; another 41 "cleared", 16 sail. Bark *Tordenskjold* arrives with bulwarks smashed and split sails after 90 days "heavy W. and W.N.W. weather" from Newcastle.

News headlines of war. "probable battle . . . Heavy Firing towards Gettysburg all Night." *Tribune*. "General Meade opening the Ball beautifully." *Herald*

Although far from attack, city almost defenceless. Garrison troops from Fort Hamilton ordered to Harrisburg, leaving 3 companies and 133 raw recruits to man outlying forts. General Wool appeals today to Brooklyn Navy-Yard. "*Roanoke* has left for Hampton Roads". Without replacement gun boats "New York will be in a defenceless condition."

Duryee's Zouaves offers $250 bounty to soldiers re-enlisting in 5th New York Volunteers. "Regiment now in camp on Staten Island." 9th Regiment enlisting on Riker's Island.

40

Lincoln's Draft Bill gives government power to conscript men aged 20 to 45; city enrolments ordered yesterday. Most New Yorkers are anti-Lincoln and unenthusiastic about the war; they oppose conscription bitterly. In 11 days' time thousands of rioters will bring the city to a halt, burning draft offices, lynching, looting.

Most patriots have volunteered already. Next month Riker's Island becomes a conscript camp—"they were unspeakable", writes Bardeen, one of the guards; often substitutes bribed "with a thousand dollars in greenbacks . . . They . . . sometimes had to wear a ball and chain, as if . . . still in the prison from which they seemed to have escaped".

HARRISBURG, PENNSYLVANIA

State capital paralysed. Colonel Thompson signals Washington that troops lack wagons: "impossible . . . to hire transportation . . . people seem disinclined to do anything . . . troops are unable to move . . . not even able to haul supplies . . ."

Out on Carlisle road, 23rd New York Volunteers, National Guard, halted since dawn in hot sun. Glittering Conedoguinet stream $\frac{1}{3}$ mile away saps discipline; most men have broken ranks to swim, scrounging farmhouse "tea whitened with real cream."

Westward, Carlisle heard "heavy firing" all day yesterday; this morning an occasional boom floats in on the wind.

MORRIS FORD, ELK RIVER, TENNESSEE

Federal drive to Chattanooga by Army of the Cumberland, under General Rosecrans, began 6 days ago. Federals found Tullahoma abandoned; one brigade has hit a Confederate rearguard defending a "planked-over railroad bridge". After 3 days' heavy rain, river banks steam in the sun. Most Confederates driven by heavy gun-fire behind a hill; some dozens pinned down amidst shell-bursts and showers of earth in a river gulley. Firing dies away; silence.

"In a lull", writes John Wyeth, 4th Alabama Cavalry, "a voice . . . said, 'Hello, boys! Let's hold up awhile and talk it over.' . . . Frank Cotton replied, 'What do you want?'

The Federal answered, 'To stop firing' . . ." Agreement reached, men in blue and grey rise from cover, talk curiously across the water. One Confederate asks if Union soldiers are short of tobacco, is told, "Not any scarcer than coffee is over there."

"The truce ended abruptly when the Union officer said, 'Look out; we will have to open fire again', . . . two Parrott guns . . . were unlimbering . . . behind us . . . in plain view of the Federals."

"At 11 a.m. the enemy opened fire . . ." reports Federal Colonel Robie, 4th Ohio Cavalry, "I . . . mounted my men and retired . . ."

BALTIMORE, MARYLAND

Western Maryland Railroad from Relay House on the Northern Central is Meade's only rail link with Baltimore, and carries no telegraph. Yesterday night locos arranged to run three-hourly with dispatches. General Haupt, commanding military railroads, working like a beaver to get up supplies. Yesterday he found the line "had no experienced officers, no water stations, sidings, turn-tables or wood" for more than "3 or 4 trains per day" while the army will need 30. He has ordered "engines and cars . . . from Alexandria, with full sets of hands . . . wood . . . buckets . . ."

11.45 a.m. Thursday

GETTYSBURG, PENNSYLVANIA

Confederate outposts on extreme right flank of Hill's corps pressing south down Seminary Ridge. From Little Round Top, Federal signallers follow their movement through binoculars.

11.45 a.m. Lt. Jerome to H.Q.: "Enemy's skirmishers are advancing from the west . . ."

11.55 a.m. "The rebels are in force, and our skirmishers give way . . . the woods are full of them."

Sun piercing the haze; a still heat. On Cemetery Hill, Coffin is offered lunch with General Howard and his staff. "The bullets were occasionally singing . . . Soldiers were . . . removing the monuments from their pedestals.

" 'If a shot should strike a stone, the pieces . . . would . . . do injury,' said the General.

"The flowers were blooming around us. I gathered a handful as a momento . . . N.W. and S.W. . . . alive with the Rebels—long lines . . . deploying . . . tents going up . . . wagons, slowly winding along the roads, reaching as far as the eye could see . . ."

Close by, S. M. Carpenter of *New York Herald* watches Gettysburg "silent as the grave. Not a voice . . . but the swallows . . . and the song of the larks . . ." A mile north, Barlow has been "moved up into another house, just inside of the town where an elderly lady and her daughter were very kind . . . I found some books there . . ."

General Schimmelfennig, XI corps, is in hiding, hungry. Trapped up a blind alley in yesterday's rout,

smashed across the head with a rifle butt, he escaped over a fence into a kitchen garden. Crawling inside a shed he "found a litter of straw . . . and other refuse . . . intended for pigs", writes Schurz.

By the western outskirts, on the Chambersburg pike, a "Lady of Gettysburg" has come up from her cellar: "tried to get something to eat. My husband went to the garden and picked a mess of beans, though stray . . . bullets . . . whizzed about his head . . . I baked a pan of shortcake and boiled a piece of ham, the last we had in the house, and some neighbours coming in . . . we had the first quiet meal since the contest began".

On Cemetery Ridge, notes Haskell, "the men stacked their arms—in long bristling rows . . . some went to sleep . . . some, a single man carrying 20 canteens slung over his shoulder, went for water. Some . . . boiled a dipper of coffee . . ."

Behind Culp's Hill, Hutchinson, XII corps, continues writing his mother:

"12 o'clock noon.

"We have been ordered up to the front . . . We are now laying in a clover field . . . The Artillery on the heights fires at intervals . . . I just took out the photographs of sister Mary & Fanny and thought how frightened they both would be could they know where their hopeful brother was . . . You do not know how much I think of you all."

Soldiers live for letters, and leave at campaign's end.

Sgt. Allen's "dear companion" is hundreds of miles away in Loogootee, Indiana. In May he wrote: "if I could get to see you and the Children it would be dance enough for me." Sgt's pay is $15 monthly, and no free fares. Allen wrote, 3 June: "it will cost a good little pile of money but . . . they have changed the furlows . . . 5 days now instead of 15 so that would not give me time enough . . ." He sent instead money, a camp photographer's "likeness taken with my uniform on", and his hopes.

WILLOUGHBY RUN VALLEY

No sign from Longstreet. Fremantle: "I rode to the extreme right with Colonel Manning . . . we ate quantities of cherries and got . . . corn for our horses . . . bathed in a small stream . . ." On Seminary Ridge, Lee has waited one dragging hour for attack to begin. All Hill's corps is ready. Ewell is ready. Bewildered, Lee at last turns back. About 12.30 p.m. he finds Longstreet, who, against direct orders, has hung on for Law's brigade. The Alabamans, parched, smothered in dust from a 24 mile tramp in 9 hours, have come up "shortly before noon" to join "the other brigades of Hood's division resting about a mile from the town", reports Law.

One last conference, perhaps heated, between Lee, Generals and staff. "Edged up as near as he dared" is a Texan private, Ferdinand Hahn. He recognizes Lee, Longstreet, Hood from his pre-war days as hotel clerk in San Antonio. After ½ hour's eavesdropping Hahn strolls back to his company.

Hood's Texan brigade is a mile off the road, down the valley. During the morning flour and rations were rumoured, and "the skillet wagon drove up and unloaded", writes Polley. "fires were built and skillet lids put on to heat . . ."

Hahn breaks the news. "You might as well quit bothering . . ."

"What have you heard, Hahn . . .?"

"Only this. I got up pretty close . . . an officer rode up, and . . . reported that the Yankees were massing troops on to Round Top. General Lee . . . said: 'Ah, well, that was to be expected. But General Meade might as well have saved himself the trouble, for we'll have it . . . before night.' That means . . . we'll have to move . . . as soon as Hood can send orders."

1 p.m. At last orders to march. Hood's division in rear, Lee riding with Longstreet in centre column to hurry things forward, McLaws's division in front with Kershaw's brigade leading, Capt. Johnston sent by Longstreet to guide Kershaw: less only Pickett's division, the whole 1st Corps of the Army of Northern Virginia trudges south towards opening battle.

1.15 p.m. Thursday

PRAIRIE NEAR LAKE TRAVERSE, DAKOTA TERRITORY

Shouted commands as 4,000 Federals prepare to break column, day's march finished. Watches show local St Paul's time, 12.15 p.m. Lt. Collins's diary: "Made 10 miles at 12 1/2 M. Good camping ground near Skunk Lake. Fine fish."

The soldiers are from Minnesota, like Marvin's countrymen a thousand miles away on Cemetery Ridge, but ordered to a very different service. Most of the 6th, 7th, 10th Minnesota Infantry, a company of 9th, 1st Mounted Rangers and 3rd Minnesota Battery of guns, under General Sibley, form an expedition with one aim, Indian killing.

For years expanding trade and emigration westward have cut into Indian lands. Since Minnesota became a Territory 14 years ago, Sioux tribes have been induced to sell almost the whole area north of the Minnesota River. In their last remaining 150 mile strip, Indians are swindled by white traders, run into debt over cheapjack goods, see their government payments taken in "expenses". Reservations on worst soil, bison slaughtered, forests cleared, game frightened off by steamers and settlers, Indian hunters shot.

Smouldering resentment blazed last August into hideous massacre at New Ulm. Rebellion crushed, 35 Sioux ringleaders were hung at Mankato, but raiders still strike. Only yesterday, in McLeod County, corpse of Amos Dustin, arrowed, tomahawked, left hand cut off, was found sitting in his cart with dead grandmother, wife and child dying. *St. Paul's Press* rages: "a single Indian, lurking in the grass . . . defies our whole system of . . . outposts".

When warlike Sioux were reported gathering again, by Devil's Lake, the Government decided to root them out, once and for all. Sibley's troops, 17 days from base, now striking open prairie, with no forage. Oscar Wall's diary, 20 June: "Nothing but prairie Slew watter to drink . . . I had to strain it between my teeth and spit the young frogs out or swollow them . . ." The 25th "found the skeletons of 6 Men at the trading Post". Tomorrow "grasshoppers are eating every thing . . ." Sgt. Ramer: "only the stiff straw of the marsh grass was left . . ."

Despite desperate bravery, Indians and families will be utterly routed at the battle of Big Mound by Sibley's troops—and guns. "for miles back the trail was marked with . . . abandoned furs, buffalo robes, bags of feathers, cooking utensils . . . in their haste to reach the Missouri River . . ." writes Collins. Sibley exults: "the bodies . . . have been left unburied . . . to be devoured by wolves . . ."

FORT ABERCROMBIE

Some 50 miles N.E. of Sibley more Minnesota troops, under Major Camp of 8th Infantry, defend trading outpost. 11 days' march from the fort, Capt. Fisk, with 60 men and 1 howitzer, escorting this year's North Overland emigration to Montana gold fields. Hundreds of hopeful settlers have read Fisk's notice: "I will . . . proceed via Forts Abercrombie, Union and Benton, to the Hell Gate passes of the Rocky Mountains . . . None should start with less than 9 months' . . . supplies. . . . Young, well broke, stubbed oxen, 2 yoke to the wagon . . . is the best team for your freight . . . Let each man take his trusty gun . . ." They will get through safely, making Bannock City 28 September.

400 miles to the S.W. another emigrant team crawling west on Central Overland trail to Oregon. "camped at noon near Platte river . . . Two wagons stalled in a mud hole . . ." *Royal Ross's journal.* Tonight "a stampede of the entire herd of cattle, 284 head . . ." Ross's party, 4 families from Council Bluffs, Omaha, have missed main body and joined Sam Creighton's freight team for protection. Ox wagons' speed down to 7 miles a day.

Westwards, Indian raids increasing; "14 head of horses and mules" today reported stolen from mail corps at Elk Mt. Station. At Denver, Colorado, Major Wynkoop ordered 2 days ago to "proceed to Camp Collins, where you will be joined by Companies B and M, 1st Colorado Cavalry, and Company I . . . proceed west on the Overland Stage Route, as far as Fort Bridger . . .for . . . safety of settlers and . . . security of the mail . . ."

CALIFORNIA

U.S. Department of the Pacific has 3,500 soldiers to hold Oregon, Nevada, Utah, and the whole of California. Mountains and desert infested with bandits, marauding Indians, and in the south, Confederate guerrillas. U.S. soldiers on patrol from Yuma have been shot near La Paz. Orders leave San Francisco today for Capt. Fitch, sweltering with 2 companies of 4th California infantry at Fort Mojave, to send a patrol into the blistering rocks of San Bernadino range to hunt the murderers. Tomorrow Colonel Curtis, at Camp Drum, near San Pedro, ordered to search all parties travelling south for arms being smuggled through Mexico "to the Southern Country."

ARIZONA

Tucson, 400 miles across the Gila desert from Fort Yuma, was an important post on the original Southern Overland, but civil war broke the mail route. Now only local stages groan through the desolate heat. Capt. Ffrench is cut off, men wasted with sickness. Wagons in yesterday "now idle . . . repairs . . . cannot be made, mechanics having left . . . no pork, bacon, or salt beef . . . without funds for nearly a year . . ." he reports on 15th.

In all territories, Indians more hostile. Wagon train came in 5 days ago to Fort Larned, Texas, minus saddles, grain sacks ripped. Next week Colonel Leavenworth "surrounded by the Arapaho, Kiowa, and Comanche Indians . . . Prompt action is needed".

Orders 2 days ago to Captain McMullen to take Company A, 1st Californian Infantry, "to Fort Thorn, . . . for active field service against the Indians . . ." Fort Wingate, New Mexico, opens its gates today to Capt. Chacon and 22 men, returned from fighting horse stealers. "Indians fought with great bravery, but . . . finally . . . fled."

Reprisals become revenge, building to wars of extermination. 60 sleeping Indians, with women and children, murdered this winter at Humboldt; next year 700 slaughtered at Sand Creek, Denver.

1.30 p.m. Thursday

HERR'S RIDGE, 3 MILES WEST OF GETTYSBURG

Down shaded lanes, blinded by yellow dust, men from South Carolina are trudging the reverse slopes of the ridge towards Marsh Creek. Kershaw's brigade has been ordered to a hidden detour. First west through woods, then south beside the glittering loops of the watercourse, then south again past Black Horse Tavern, now up a fenced road in the glaring heat of open fields. As they breast a hill, leading skirmishers pause: before them 3 miles of rolling country as far as the Round Tops, where Federal signal flags flicker in the sunlight.

A mile or so in rear, Lee has bidden Longstreet farewell and is riding past Pitzer's farm to join Hill at a central vantage point on Seminary Ridge.

McLaws, halting his column, rides to the front and then off the road with Colonel Johnston to explore a way hidden from the enemy signal station. Returning unsuccessful, he meets Longstreet and shows him the crest. He tells Longstreet he has in fact, on his own initiative, found a different route during the morning, but it means going back. Longstreet agrees: "then all right . . ." Cursing men reverse in their tracks.

From Little Round Top, Federal binoculars spot the glitter of muskets. Capt. Hall to Meade: "1.30 p.m. . . . enemy's infantry, about 10,000 strong, is moving from opposite our extreme left towards our right."

Kershaw's men march back a full mile, past their start lines, and meet Hood's division head on. Another halt. Longstreet suggests letting Hood take the lead, but McLaws insists on the honour of his 1st division. His men thread the length of Hood's column, files broken by the narrow lane. Whole corps begins a second detour, of 4 miles: first north, then east across the ridge by Harman's farm, then back south alongside Willoughby Run. Clouds of churned dust choke the route; men gasp in rising heat.

About 2 p.m. Longstreet rides up to McLaws: "How are you going in?" McLaws replies it depends on what he finds facing him. Longstreet assures him: "There is nothing in your front; you will be entirely on the flank of the enemy." McLaws says he will march in company columns, then face left to attack. "Old Pete" growls: "That suits me!" and rides away.

TANEYTOWN ROAD

Behind Cemetery Ridge, field on field of white canvas wagon tops—main Federal artillery and H.Q. park. Surgeons have chosen barns, sited corps' hospital tents, await supplies. Major Bush, of the Sanitary Commission: "Found our wagons early in the afternoon." Unloading "concentrated beef-soup, stimulants, crackers, condensed milk, concentrated coffee . . .shirts . . . blankets . . . bandages . . ." 2 wagons emptied, Bush prepares to ride to Westminster, for train for

Washington, to order more.

SOUTH CEMETERY RIDGE

On low ground where the ridge joins the Round Tops, III corps holds extreme Federal flank. Hunt, artillery chief, admits to Sickles that a higher position, $\frac{3}{4}$ mile in front, around a peach orchard on the Emmitsburg road, would be better for guns, and possibly for defence. But the longer line, a salient, would need more troops than Sickles's to link it with the rest of the army. Sickles presses to be allowed forward; Hunt refuses: "Not on my authority", but rides off to ask Meade. Sickles's skirmishers have already met enemy fire from woods beyond the road; crackle of musketry increases; Sickles feels trapped, on poor ground, arguments ignored.

He takes a dangerous decision . . .

At 2.15 an extraordinary sight amazes watchers on Cemetery Ridge. III corps is moving forward.

Gibbon: "long lines of battle . . . taking up position along the Emmitsburg road, batteries going into position . . ."

Haskell: "It was magnificent to see those 10 or 12 thousand men . . . cavalry upon the left flank . . .flags streaming, sweep steadily down the slope, across the valley, and up the next ascent . . ."

Within 20 minutes the advance is completed. II corps, with its own flank left dangling, wonders what on earth it can mean.

Coffin, touring eagerly, rides to "the house of Mr. Codori, on the Emmitsburg Road . . . pickets of both armies were lying in the wheat-field . . ." From a brook behind Rogers's house—only 600 yards from Lee—he finds soldiers "filling their canteens". Capt. Blake, 11th Massachusetts: "cows . . . grazing . . . tame pigeons sat upon the dovecots . . . the lady . . . in the cottage was baking bread, and sold chickens . . ."

With the next regiment, 1st Massachusetts, 15-year-old Bardeen is "in the limbs of a tree . . . writing in the very green diary . . . we could see the Confederate wagon trains and artillery moving to our left . . . an officer on a white horse . . . rode up and down far in front . . . I wondered whether he had anybody at home to care whether he was killed or not".

About 2.50 p.m. Gibbon, on Cemetery Ridge: "Noticing . . . beyond the Peach Orchard . . . a body of timber, I turned to General Hancock and asked: 'Do you suppose the enemy has anything in that wood?' The words were scarcely uttered when out of the timber, puff after puff of smoke was seen . . ."

3 p.m. Thursday

FREDERICK, MARYLAND

Beyond 5 miles from Gettysburg, hardly anyone yet sure where Lee is. Federal garrison troops tramping Baltimore and Ohio railtracks towards Frederick; behind them Harper's Ferry on the Potomac lies abandoned. Fearing overwhelming attack, General French prepares 2 regiments to cover the Monocacy rail bridges tonight.

Harrisburg, Pennsylvania, seething. Governor Curtis's train chugging in from Philadelphia "where he addressed the citizens" for volunteers. Railways now under military control, "no movements of cars or engines . . . without . . . authority", reports Colonel Thompson. Near Carlisle, trackmen, abandoning repairs to the Cumberland line, "had to return with their tools . . . rebels on both sides of the Railroad . . ." *Herald*

In Tennessee, Cumberland Mountains soaked by rain. Major Connolly, on reconnaissance with 123rd Illinois Regiment for General Rosecrans, found yesterday only dry day in a week: "we lived in the rain, slept in the mud . . . as wet as fish . . ." 19th Michigan is Federal rearguard, "following up the main army" writes Sgt. Griffis next Sunday. "It rains everry day . . . wheat fawling to the ground for want of hands to harvest it . . ."

Confederate Chattanooga, in line of advance, buzzing with rumours. Nurse Kate Cumming's diary, yesterday: "News . . . that the enemy is across the river, and intends shelling . . . having hospital flags put up . . . but . . . it is said the enemy pay no respect to them . . . packing up in a hurry to move."

LOWER MISSISSIPPI

Across the border of Illinois swelters "delectable Cairo", shanty-town river port of mud. Coffin: "all the filth and slime of this world . . . debris of everything . . ." Rosecrans has asked for gunboats on the Tennessee river, to cut any Confederate retreat south by Florence or Decatur crossings. Telegraph "lines are down and I am trying to reach the gunboats in another way", reported Capt. Pennock yesterday. "We are at work on the *Paw Paw* and *Peosta* . . ."

Between Cairo and Vicksburg, 350 air miles south, defences wide open to a Confederate thrust from Arkansas. General Hurlbut reported from Memphis last week that enemy "at Jacksonport . . . building 60 deep flat-boats on Black River". Today an enemy deserter reports: "Price is moving south, and will make an attempt on Helena . . ." Hurlbut warns troops downriver to keep lines "rigidly closed". Deserter says Confederate "women are used as spies".

From Memphis naval yards *Tyler* gunboat, repaired, today steams for Helena. *Bragg* still under workmen. Downstream, a boarding party seizes steamer *Eureka*, found 20 miles below limit of its permit, suspected blockade runner. Commander Phelps unearths "empty tin boxes . . . stowed in the run with loose cotton . . . suitable for smuggling quinine . . ."

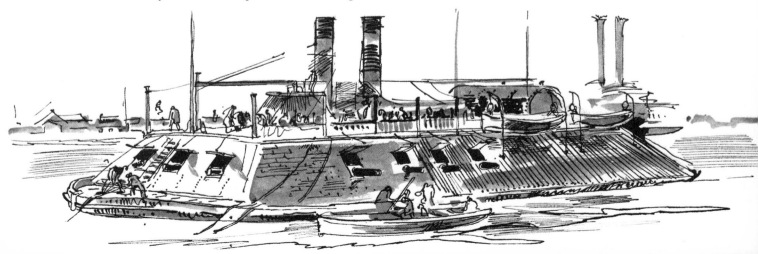

YAZOO RIVER, NEAR VICKSBURG

Drowsy heat; 2 p.m. local time. At Snyder's Bluff, Chauncey Cooke, home-sick for far-off Wisconsin, is writing his father. The lumbering *Dexter* yesterday brought back his unit from a 200 mile sortie upriver to Cypress Bend. On entering the Mississippi, he writes, "Soon as we got fairly into the current, the boys made a rush for the boiler deck to get a drink of the water that came from the lakes . . . of Wisconsin . . . we saw dead mules and cattle floating by . . . but . . . we drank, and drank, until it ran out of our nose just because it came from the glorious North."

Last Sunday they landed on the Arkansas shore. A large plantation searched for enemy guerrillas revealed only hoof marks, slaves, and 3 white women. "One pleaded pitifully . . . urging us to stay out . . . at times screaming as if her heart was breaking. She said her mother was sick and likely to die . . . One of the boys pushed by . . . and opened a closet . . . but we found nothing but dresses . . . and blankets. I got ashamed and wished that I was out of it . . . I . . . found a book-case. I stuck Longfellow's *Hiawatha* in my pocket . . .

"When I went outside I found several buildings on fire. The orders had been not to set any fires, but nobody cared . . ."

TEXAS

Countless Confederate plantations abandoned in the war zone. Approaching Lamar county, one refugee wagon pulls out from noon halt. Kate Stone's family fled Brockenburn, cotton estate of 1,200 acres, when U.S. troops invaded the area, N.W. of Vicksburg, last March. 300 miles, with baggage lost, by boat, train, finally 3 weeks by wagon. Rain all this week "ruining most of the clothes . . . we have . . . ticks, redbugs, fleas by the millions, and snakes . . . Game, deer and turkeys, are abundant . . . but . . . too tough to eat . . . at night when we stopped, I had only spirit to . . . watch Annie get supper or to look up at the stars and think of all the dear friends . . . sweeping farther and farther away . . ." Journey's end within 3 days, at "a rough two-room shanty with the overseer and his family . . . we must needs make the best of it". *Kate Stone's diary*

BALTIMORE, MARYLAND

Clattering hooves, stable-boys running, at Adam's Express Company. Rising to the glory of the famed Pony Express to California, killed by opening of Pacific telegraph 2 years ago. Despite herculean efforts, Western Maryland Railroad remains hopelessly inadequate to carry supplies, let alone regular express locos with dispatches, as promised. Superintendent Shoemaker's telegram to Washington, received 3.45 p.m.:

"have organised a horse express from this point . . . 1st . . . will leave in half an hour . . . next at 6 p.m. . . . we have . . . expressmen extending from Westminster to General Meade's H.Q. . . . the line from here to Westminster is now being put on."

3 p.m. Thursday

GETTYSBURG, PENNSYLVANIA

At H.Q., Meade finishes dictating a report to General-in-Chief Halleck in Washington. "I have concentrated my army . . . the enemy . . . has been moving on both my flanks, apparently . . . I . . . will endeavour to act with caution." He signs the pad; a staff officer inscribes the time: 3 p.m.

Meade then sends aides to summon all corps commanders to H.Q.

WILLOUGHBY RUN VALLEY

Strung along some 3 miles of footpath and lane, interminable columns of Longstreet's corps at last nearing their assault line. In front, Kershaw's brigade has left the run by the school house near Pitzer's, and is tramping the last lap direct towards the Round Tops. Kershaw: "At 3 p.m. the head of my column emerged from the woods, and came into the open field in front of the stone wall . . . by Flaherty's farm, and . . . past Snyder's."

For 2 hours the whole corps has been marching blind. Now, as regiment after regiment crosses Seminary Ridge, they meet the absolutely unexpected: close range cannon fire. Flashes from Want's peach orchard are barely ½ mile off; other Federal guns open up from the S.E. So far from being undefended, Cemetery Ridge shows the glint of bayonets almost to the Round Tops.

Kershaw: "in full view of the Federal position . . . I immediately formed line of battle along the stone wall . . . under cover of my skirmishers . . . near the Emmitsburg road."

McLaws rides up, is taken on foot to the skirt of trees. "the view astonished me, as the enemy was massed in my front, and extended to my right and left as far as I could see". Under fire, divisional artillery, Cabell's

battalion, is manhandled up on Kershaw's right, on to high ground near Snyder's.

3.20 p.m. Law's Alabamans have marched 28 miles in 12 hours. Nearly dropping, they lead Hood's division into the torrid heat of an open plateau behind Flaherty's woods. Federal guns begin to tear gaps in their columns.

Couriers galloping. McLaws's troops aligned, ready "an order came from General Longstreet . . . asking why I did not charge . . ." McLaws points to the enemy strength, says he must have time to prepare a strong assault. Again the order, again McLaws explains. A third time, "peremptorily". Then "I got on my horse and sent word that in five minutes I would be under way." Finally "a courier dashed up . . . for me to wait until Hood got into position".

Longstreet has altered plans. Hood's division will march another mile south, behind McLaws, to try to outflank the enemy. Hood will begin the attack, driving up the Emmitsburg road; McLaws will follow when Hood reaches his front.

Artillery fire increases. Cabell's batteries reply to Federal guns in peach orchard.

MEADE'S H.Q., CEMETERY RIDGE

3.25 p.m. Nearly all corps commanders gathered. General Gouverneur Warren, Chief of Engineers, enters with astounding news. Sickles's III corps is way out of line, not even linked with II, its left flank floating. While Warren speaks, cannon fire and musketry swells from the S.W.

Meade at once sends Warren to look at the Round Tops, orders Sykes to march up V corps fast, and says he will meet them on the field.

3.30 p.m. Thursday

VICKSBURG, MISSISSIPPI

A scorched, bone dry valley. 2.30 p.m. local time. One weary column, part of a Confederate relief force trailing the dirt roads near Brownsville, passed a girl in a carriage this morning. "I have thought of her twenty times today . . . through the heat and dust and almost dying of thirst." *Robert Patrick's diary*

3 days ago Charles Haydon, 2nd Michigan, tramped dust "full 4 inches deep, fine & light as flour. . . . The heat reflected . . . seems to scorch like a blaze of fire. . . . Magnolias . . . in full bloom . . . Peaches seem to grow wild. Fig trees . . . loaded with green fruit".

When not drained by dysentery, Federal bellies are full. At Snyder's Bluff, 2 weeks ago, Chauncey Cooke saw "Men shooting cattle running wild . . . Ten miles from here the people in Vicksburg are starving . . . and where we are camped the air is poisoned with the decaying flesh of animals more than we can eat. What a world this is . . ."

Around the beleagured city, Confederate perimeter under non-stop shelling. General Bowen warns today: "Our position on the Jackson road is fast becoming more dangerous. The enemy have a Cohorn mortar and our exact range." Men lining the huge crater breached by yesterday's mine are of 1st Missouri Infantry. Their colonel, Cockrell, reports "this terrific explosion threw . . . the 6th Missouri . . . back . . . over the brow of the hill . . .but . . . these gallant soldiers rallied . . . and

rushed back . . . veterans of the 3rd Louisiana Infantr raised a cheer". 11 men were killed, 83 wounded.

Half starved, weakened by 45 days and night in cramped, exposed trenches, defenders barely hope "I have a newspaper . . . published . . . on wall paper. wrote Major Simons in his diary yesterday. "I have als made two little charmes out of minnie balls for m little pet, how I wish I could see the dear loved ones bu I must wate."

General John Pemberton commands all Vicksburg defences. As long as the garrison holds out, Federal cannot control the lower Mississippi; once surrendered Port Hudson would follow and open the whol valley. On 19 May, Pemberton signalled Richmon for a "large force", failing which "Vicksburg befor long must fall"; but help never came. 30,000 soldier and a city of civilians have all but consumed store that began the siege. One million cartridges lac caps. Houses are shattered; a week ago townspeopl dug earth caves to escape shelling. Bread raw, half pe meal. Mule flesh has been tried, found eatable. Som wit has written a menu:

Hotel De VICKSBURG
Bill of fare for July 1863
ROAST Mule sirloin . . . ENTREES Mule head stuffed a la mode . . . SIDE DISHES Mule salad . . . JELLIES Mule foot . . . LIQUORS Missis sippi Water, vintage of 1492 . . .
Humour hides despair. 2 weeks ago a courier slippe

PORT HUDSON, LOUISIANA

In one gulley, $\frac{1}{2}$ mile outside main fort, a sunlit hell. Rubber groundsheets hang from splintered saplings; wounded lie sheltered in a narrow fold of earth; soldiers huddle asleep; riflemen motionless behind a log barrier at the lower mouth of the gulley. A mortar shell bursts, showering gravel; occasionally a minnie ball whines. 36th day in a "wilderness of death" for 12th Connecticut Volunteers. Since 1st Union assault failed, Capt. De Forest's regiment has held this "detestable" position, entirely exposed to fire from the fort. "There was but one spot . . . where bullets never struck . . . it rarely fell to . . . my company . . . I used to look with . . . longing at this nasty but wholesome patch . . . 30 ft long by 10 ft broad . . ." writes De Forest. On average, 3 men killed or wounded every 2 days.

Beyond the parapet, invisible now behind an earthwork, lie the Confederates, "sallow, darkly sunburnt men" who "stared back . . . in grim silence" during a truce 6 weeks ago. 12th Connecticut is in 3 duty parties, each spending 1 day at the parapet, 2 days off. Enemy breastwork is close: "our men sighted it on their Enfields as 150 yards, but it did not look so far . . ." Through notched loopholes, "with the patience of cats . . . the men would peer for hours . . . for a chance to shoot a Rebel . . . Several of our men were shot in the face . . . as they were taking aim . . . It was . . . lazy, monotonous, sickening, murderous . . ."

Half a century hence, other men, under a European sun, will lie much like this across the length of France.

out to contact Johnston's relief army; Johnston advised surrender; but the courier was captured returning. Pemberton has had no word. On Monday "Many Soldiers" signed a warning to the general: "Sir . . . Our rations . . . down to one biscuit and a small bit of bacon per day . . . If you can't feed us, you had better surrender us . . . I tell you plainly, men are not going to lie and perish . . . This army is now ripe for mutiny, unless it can be fed."

Yesterday Pemberton asked whether the men's strength would stand a break-out attempt. Simons thinks it impossible; his diary, yesterday: "the men have been in the trenches for so long a time on short rations . . . no exercise all the time . . . I do not think they could now march four miles . . ." General Hébert reports officially: "the spirit of my men to fight is unbroken, but their bodies are worn out".

Simons, today: "I have almost given up the last hope of our being releaved, I have been fixing a box in which to put my papers & bury them . . . the Yankees shall not have the sattesfaction of looking over them, I will put this book in the box and hope some day to get possession of it . . . I feel truly sad; all looks dark and gloomy ahead."

Tomorrow Pemberton asks for a truce, meets Grant, accepts generous terms. Saturday 29,376 officers and men lay down arms, free then to return to their homes, on parole that they will not serve again in the war.

3.35 p.m. Thursday

SOUTHERN SEMINARY RIDGE, GETTYSBURG

Law's brigade clears the last fringe of wood near Snyder's house and, marching south, begins crossing the Emmitsburg road. Law: "Round Top rose like a huge sentinel guarding the Federal left . . . puffs of smoke rising at intervals along the line of hills . . ." Just how far do the Federals stretch? As his men form line, Law sends off "six picked men as scouts . . . to the summit of [Big] Round Top" to find out.

3.40 p.m. Texan brigade, under General Robertson, now off the plateau, continues the line northwards. John West, 4th Texas: "we came into line in the edge of timber . . . I could see the Federal batteries . . . by the smoke . . . We stood in column of fours, with our faces towards our right . . . the first shot . . . passed by on a bound over us, scattering dust and dirt . . . The next . . . passed . . . beyond us . . . The third shot hit our line about eight feet in front of me, knocking off one soldier's head and cutting another in two, bespattering us with blood .

"Just then we fronted to the left . . ."

Hood's artillery unlimbers along the edge of trees, and opens. ½ mile north, Longstreet and staff have reached corps centre. McLaws's left brigade, General Barksdale's, is only 500 yards from enemy guns in peach orchard, opposite. Ross is with Longstreet: "As we passed Barksdale's Mississippi Brigade the General came up eagerly to Longstreet, 'I wish you would let me go in General; I would take that battery in 5 minutes.' 'Wait a little,' said Longstreet, 'we are all going in presently.'"

BALTIMORE PIKE

2 miles away, beyond Cemetery Ridge, Sykes has gained his H.Q., issued orders. Regiment after regiment of V corps, rifles shouldered, tramp off on their support march towards the ridge.

LITTLE ROUND TOP

Warren has reached the summit. It is undefended; only some signallers. If the Top falls, enemy cannon could sweep the length of Cemetery Ridge—and the Union army. It is "the key to the whole position", writes Warren. He sends a message for a Federal battery, way downhill in Devil's Den, to fire into the woods near Snyder's. The sound causes Law's men involuntarily to turn their heads; Warren sees "the glittering of . . . bayonets . . . far outflanking . . . any of our troops . . ." Appalled at the sight, he scribbles a message by courier to Meade "to send a division at least . . ."

At army H.Q., conference broken up by 3.55. Meade, mounting the first horse at hand, sees Sickles arriving. "Don't dismount; I'll follow you", shouts Meade.

SEMINARY RIDGE

4 p.m. Longstreet's corps in position: support brigades in rear, assault brigades with regiments in double lines. To the north, Hill's corps; beyond the town, Ewell's. A 5 mile curve, waiting.

I corps artillery will fire a barrage of 15 minutes. Hood's division will then attack; Cabell's gunners will later "fire 3 guns in rapid succession" as signal for McLaws's; other divisions to follow in succession northwards.

Kershaw: "In my center-front was a stone farmhouse . . . Behind . . . a morass . . . Beyond the morass was a stony hill, covered with heavy timber and . . . bowlders . . . I determined to move upon the stony hill . . . with my center . . ."

On the south wing, Law has incredible news. Skirmishers have captured some lightly wounded Federals "going to the rear" from the "medical train behind the mountain. . . . They also stated", says Law, "that the . . . trains were insecurely guarded", and that "a good farm road" leads around the Tops to the area. About 4.10 one of Law's scouts gets back, reporting "no Federal force on the summit" of Big Round Top.

Law gallops to Hood. A flank attack might crumple the whole Union army. But advance as ordered, up the Emmitsburg road, will only entangle men in boulders and gulleys skirting the Round Tops, expose them to murderous fire from Cemetery Ridge while clearing the peach orchard, and mean heavy losses before reaching the Cemetery proper.

Hood agrees, send a staff captain urgently to Longstreet. The reply is unyielding: "Lee's orders are to attack up the Emmitsburg road." Hood sends again, even a third time. Longstreet's rankling bitterness rejects every appeal. Lee wanted this attack; this attack he will have—exactly as ordered. . . .

PEACH ORCHARD

A short lull. Meade, grim faced, is riding with Sickles towards his lines. "General Sickles," he rasps, "I am afraid you are too far out."

Suddenly a shattering roar, a ripple of gun flashes, runs from Snyder's north. In town, Professor Jacobs looks at his watch: "at 20 minutes past 4 p.m. the enemy began . . . a terrific artillery fire . . ." Barrage has begun.

Federal batteries reply; gunners begin dropping among the peach trees; smoke cuts the view. Sickles, confidence slipping, sees his troops almost surrounded. "I will withdraw if you wish, Sir."

"I wish to God you could," barks Meade, "but those people won't let you."

4.25 p.m. Thursday

FIELDS NEAR PEACH ORCHARD, GETTYSBURG

Sickles's guns came in position an hour since, Capt. Clark's battery and Capt. Ames's, from army artillery reserve, under fire. 3 more reserve batteries ordered up by Hunt now going into action. Teams working under the bombardment, manhandling 12 pdr Napoleon smoothbores off the road, aligning barrels by trail hand-spikes, levelling bushes and fences in front. Limbers unhooked, some horses still yoked to spare caissons. Numbers 1, alongside sponge buckets, ramming woollen cartridge bag and wad, then solid shot. Numbers 3 with friction primer; 6 laying out shells and fuses for short range fire later. Open sights set at maximum, 1,500 yards, 5° elevation.

Clark's Battery B, 1st New Jersey, on the exposed ridge of the cross-roads. "a spherical case shot", writes Michael Hanifen, "exploded to the right of the first caisson . . . A fragment of shell disembowelled the nigh pole horse; another took off his foreleg . . . the team started to run . . ."

Near Devil's Den, Hunt sees that Capt. Smith's battery, 10 pdr rifled Parrotts, is silent. Leaving his horse, he begins the steep climb on foot to their crest.

Other Federal guns finding their targets. Westwards, Alexander controls Longstreet's artillery. "The ground at Cabell's position gave little protection, and he suffered rapidly . . . I ran up Huger with 18 guns of my own 26, to Warfield's house, within 500 yards of Peach Orchard . . . This made 54 guns in action . . . but . . . so accurate was the enemy's fire, that 2 of my guns were fairly dismounted, and the loss of men was so great that I had to ask General Barksdale . . . for help to handle the heavy 24 pdr howitzers . . ."

The cannonade rages from Snyder's to Culp's Hill. Fremantle: "A dense smoke arose for 6 miles. There was little wind . . . Every now and then a caisson would blow up . . . General Lee joined Hill just below our tree . . . looking through his fieldglass . . . generally he sat quite alone on the stump of a tree . . . a Confederate band . . . began to play polkas and waltzes . . ."

WEIKART'S WOODS, NEAR LITTLE ROUND TOP

Sykes's V corps, with 20 extra cartridges per man, ha marched over Cemetery Ridge, and formed behind a large wheatfield in reserve to III corps. Men strugglin; up through the trees with refilled water bottles. Jame Houghton, 4th Michigan: "no springs to be found nearby was a ditch that had some stagnate water in i we poaked the Skum one side with our cups the gave the water a spat to scare the bugs and wiglers t the bottom then filled our canteens . . ."

Barrage at its height, 1st division is moving forward Sykes's staff party reconnoitring ahead, when an en gineer officer gallops up with a desperate appeal from Warren. Despite messages to Meade and to Sickles Little Round Top, looming ½ mile south, is still bar of troops.

Sykes immediately sends back an aide. Leadin; brigade is Colonel Strong Vincent's. Bugler Olive Norton, carrying the brigade flag, hears the aide shout ing for the divisional commander, General Barnes Vincent senses the urgency in the courier's voice, de mands to be given the orders direct. Learning th danger, he says he will take his men to Little Roun Top on his own responsibility. Ordering Colonel Jame Rice, 44th New York, to bring the regiments "at th double quick" he gallops straight for the hill. Nortor follows, pennant streaming.

Their horses, stumbling among loose stones, mak no headway up the steep N.W. face. "Skirting th northern foot of the ridge" they circle the hill to com up through the trees on the eastern slope. Above them huge boulders rise a sheer 50 feet to Warren's summit in front, the flattish spur seems to end abruptly agains the smoke of bombardment, eastwards.

A mile north, Haskell on Cemetery Ridge: "All wa astir now on our crest. . . . the men were all in thei places, and you might have heard the rattle of 10,00 ramrods as they . . . 'thugged' upon the little globes an cones of lead."

Gaining his hill-top, Hunt finds Smith's guns haule by rope and handspike "one by one, over the rocks" o to the summit. Opening up, they come under heav fire. "Telling him he would probably lose his battery' Hunt scrambles down the slope to call up infantry, nearly trampled by stampeding cattle. "A shell ha exploded in . . . one of them . . . others were torn an wounded . . . bellowing and rushing in their terror . . .

EMMITSBURG ROAD, BELOW SNYDER'S

4.35 p.m. After 15 minutes artillery duel, dense smok blankets the whole valley.

Law's and Robertson's brigades aligned, Benning' and Anderson's 200 yards in rear. Lt. John Oates, wea from sickness, crawls to his company in 15th Alabam;

efusing to be left behind. He tells his brother, regimental colonel, "No, sir, I am an officer . . . I shall go through . . ." All Colonel Oates's men heat stricken, esperate for drinking water. "Two men from each of he eleven companies" sent with "all the canteens to a ell about one hundred yards in our rear" not yet back.

Sharp orders bring the exhausted men to their feet. agged, many shoeless, they line off shoulder to houlder from company captains as right markers. econd rank a pace behind. Colour bearers with regimental flags in centre of regiments. Rifles loaded, artridge pouches unbuttoned, bayonets fixed. For this noment men have tramped Virginia, Maryland, half ennsylvania. Thirst and aching muscles forgotten, erves fluttering, they face front. Fields, fences, rocks, hine with strange clarity; under the blinding sun ederal gun flashes seem terribly near.

4.40 p.m. Thursday

EMMITSBURG ROAD, WEST OF GETTYSBURG

Longstreet rides up to Hood, silencing one last protest against the form of attack: "We must obey the orders of General Lee."

John West: "a short pause. I saw General Hood . . . about 300 or 400 yards obliquely to my left . . . He took his hat, held it above him . . . rose to his full height in his stirrups, and shouted . . . 'Forward! steady; forward!' . . . I heard the word passing down the line, 'Quick, but not double quick!'"

Under shouted orders, long grey ranks begin to walk steadily down the sloping fields. Regiment after regiment moves off, taking up the line leftwards. Deafened by Longstreet's guns now firing overhead from the ridge behind; bracketed by Federal batteries finding their range. At 300 yards 1st rail fence climbed, torn down. Another at 600 yards.

Law's right heading for Big Round Top, due east. 3rd Arkansas, the division's left, has been ordered to hug the Emmitsburg road north. Gaps open. Oates: "our division was spread out like . . . a half-open fan . . ." Law orders the 48th and 44th Alabama to flank leftwards, tells Oates he is now the right, and to skirt the base of Big Round Top.

4.46 p.m. Ahead a stone wall by Slyder's. Behind it a single blue line of the most forward Union outposts. A curl of smoke; 2nd U.S. Sharpshooters fires the 1st Federal volley. Without pausing to return the fire, Confederates walk on.

4.50. Vincent reaches the spur of Little Round Top, and under shellfire scrambles down on foot among the boulders to select regimental positions.

4.55. Extreme right of Confederate advance now only ¾ mile S.W. of Vincent. Union sharpshooters falling back sideways on to Big Round Top, firing steadily. Colonel Oates, 15th Alabama, finds "no one in my rear or on my right" to meet this flank threat. "I gave the command to change direction to the right. The 7 companies of the 47th swung around with the 15th and kept in line . . ." Oates's men heading straight for Big Round Top.

Rest of Law's brigade, mixed with Robertson's, nearing a stream and low marsh leading to Devil's Den. Federal guns and musketry seem on all sides. Past the stream rougher ground, more rocks. James Bradfield, 1st Texas: "'Forward—double quick,' rang out, and then Texas turned loose. . . . every man for himself. . . . my right file man, William Langley . . . fell against me . . . dead. . . . that same familiar 'spat' . . . sounded near, and . . . I saw Bose Perry double over . . . He . . . came on, dragging his wounded leg, and firing as he advanced."

Sickles's skirmishers retire uphill towards Smith's battery above Devil's Den. Smith's guns blazing at

400 yards range. Law directs the 44th Alabama to swing left against them, through a gloomy defile. Colonel Perry: "rocks, from 6 to 15 feet high . . . among them winding passages carpeted with moss. . . . a cavernous coolness pervades the air . . ." Union batteries almost overhead seem to Perry "a volcano in eruption". Then "a sheet of flame burst from the rocks less than 50 yards away".

5 p.m. Another change in direction. 4 regiments, the 4th and 48th Alabama, 5th and 4th Texas, turn right towards the south slope of Little Round Top in a race to occupy its heights.

Union infantry, Vincent's brigade, scrambling up the reverse slopes. Colonel Chamberlain, 20th Maine: "The enemy's artillery got range of our column as we were climbing the spur, and the crashing of the shells among the rocks . . . made us move lively . . ." From the crest, Gerrish sees "Sickles' corps . . . enveloped in . . . a vast window of fire." As the 4 regiments run up, Vincent orders them into a crescent, with skirmishers forward into the valley.

5.5 p.m. Confederates finding the wooded valley steeper and rougher. John West: "boulders from the size of a hogshead to . . . a small house". Colonel Bryan, 5th Texas: "huge rocks forming defiles through which no more than 3 or 4 men could pass abreast . . ."

Barely in position, Vincent's outposts open fire on the grey masses below them. Nearly a mile from start lines, exhausted Confederates try to form for an uphill charge. Val Giles, 4th Texas: "our brigade got 'jammed'. Regiments overlapped . . . Confusion . . . everywhere . . . Hood . . . shot from his horse. Robertson, our brigadier . . . carried from the field. Colonel Powell . . . riddled with bullets . . . Colonel Carter . . . lay dying . . . Every fellow was his own general". Texans have come under their own shellfire. "our artillery . . . cutting its fuse too short. The shells were bursting behind us, in the treetops, over our heads . . ."

5.10 p.m. Hood's left wing grinding to a halt before the ridge west of Devil's Den. McLaws's division has not advanced in support. 3rd Arkansas pinned by flank fire from peach orchard, 1st Texas twice halted. Law throws in reserve brigades, Benning's and Anderson's, for all-out attack.

2 miles away, beyond Cemetery Ridge, Charles Benton, lying waiting with part of Federal XII corps, hears "on the sultry smoke-laden air . . . a new and peculiar sound; a prolonged, fierce, wavering yell, gaining in strength and rising higher and higher until it finally died away in a scream.

" 'What's that?' I enquired of a veteran.

" 'Oh, that's the "Rebel yell",' he answered, 'they're charging now; listen.' . . . the sound of musketry broke out thicker and louder; the roar of artillery increased . . ."

5.15 p.m. Thursday

Northern apex of Meade's position. Federal guns of I and XI corps massed almost wheel to wheel in and around the hilltop cemetery, engaging Ewell's batteries north of town, 1400 yards away.

Colonel Wainwright: "the enemy planted 4 twenty-pounder and 6 ten-pounder Parrotts on a high knoll opposite . . . I was able to reply with 13 three-inch guns, so that the weight of metal was about equal . . . the rebel guns . . . were on higher ground . . . some 30 yards apart, while ours were not over 12; and . . . the limbers stood absolutely crowded together.

"a single twenty-pounder shot . . . struck . . . a line of infantry who were lying down beside the wall. Taking the line lengthways, it literally ploughed up 2 or 3 yards of men . . . a shell which burst directly under Cooper's left gun, killed one man outright, blew another all to pieces . . . The man . . . lost his right hand, his left arm at the shoulder, and his ribs so broken open that you ould see right into him . . . Cooper came to me and asked permission for his brother, who was their bugler, to go and remain with him while he lived. . . .

"Cooper's and Reynolds's batteries fired beautifully .. Wiedrich . . . made wretched work of it : his Germans were all excitement . . . I had to go to each piece myself, set their pendulum haussée, and show them just what length of fuse to use."

Minute after minute Union and Confederate guns hammer relentlessly. Wainwright: "Still we were able to . . . drive them from the field in about 2 hours . . . they left 28 dead horses . . ."

5.30 p.m. 2 miles south, beyond Meade's left flank, Confederates pressing a desperate mountain assault. For ½ hour past, 15th and 47th Alabama hauling themselves by finger-tip up the face of Big Round Top, catching to the rocks and bushes and crawling over the boulders . . . the enemy . . . kept retreating . . . firing down on us . . ." writes Oates. Spread-eagled on burning ironstone, blinded by sweat and dust, his men near collapse from lack of water. Detail with refilled bottles lost behind. "Some of my men fainted from heat, exhaustion, and thirst."

Northwestwards, reserve brigades crammed right and left of 1st Texas and 3rd Arkansas, a screaming Confederate mass gains the crest of Devil's Den. Law, divisional commander since Hood's wound, finds, 50 minutes after first advancing, no support whatever on his left. He gallops back ¾ miles to the Confederate woods, to Longstreet's start line. "I found McLaws still . . . there, his troops suffering considerably from severe fire . . . from the opposite hills . . . Kershaw . . . had not yet received the order to move." Law excitedly points out his left flank, threatened by the whole of Sickles's peach orchard salient.

5.40. While they argue, 3 separate guns boom their signal. Kershaw: "the men leaped over the wall and were promptly aligned; the word was given, and the brigade moved off . . . Longstreet accompanied me . . . on foot, as far as the Emmitsburg road. All . . . officers were dismounted . . ." Again a failure of staff orders. When we were about the Emmitsburg road, I heard Barksdale's drums beat the assembly, and knew *then* that I should have no immediate support on my left . . . The 2nd and 8th South Carolina regiments were then moving majestically across the fields . . . with the steadiness of troops on parade."

Kershaw's centre marching for a bare hill on the peach orchard road, the inner hinge of Sickles's salient. Left regiments, 3rd and 7th South Carolina, wheel left towards Federal guns blazing from the peach trees. Mistaken orders halt them, exploding grape and canister at close range cut swathes in their ranks.

5.45 p.m. Barksdale's Mississippi brigade charges across the smoking valley straight for the orchard. Capt. Lamar sees the general, white hair streaming, "as far as the eye could follow, still ahead of his men, leading them on . . ." Kershaw's men storm their hill.

Sickles's left flank regiments, faces blackened by powder, reloading, firing, steadily pressed back. To their rear, leading brigades of V corps standing in line by regiment, in woods masking a wheatfield.

Houghton: "a battery . . . was feading the Rebbels with grape and canister . . . bullets were whizzing buzing and spatting all around us. we were ordered to lye down as we could do no firing while there was other troops in front . . . frequently wounded men passing by us telling us to go in and give them hel".

5.50. Oates's Alabamans gained Big Round Top some 5 minutes ago; prostrate on the summit. Oates: "I saw Gettysburg through the foliage of the trees. Saw the smoke and heard the roar of battle . . ." A staff officer from Law rides up the other side, with orders for an immediate assault on Little Round Top, opposite. Oates argues his fantastic position, the highest point of a precipice dominating the whole battlefield. If guns could be hauled up the easier eastern slope, they could shell not only Little Round Top but the whole Union ridge beyond. "Within half an hour I could convert it into a Gibraltar." The officer half agrees, but Confederate guns are distant, trees would hinder their fire, and anyway "he had no authority to change . . . orders". Oates accepts, gives the signal to descend.

5.55. Barksdale's Mississippi regiments smash clean through 2 wood fences, drive straight into the peach orchard angle, and dislodge the 1st Federal line with the bayonet.

Haskell, from Cemetery Ridge: "amid the heavier smoke . . . now began . . . the countless flashes, and the long fiery sheets of the muskets . . . We see the long gray lines come sweeping down . . ." Federal reinforcements from II corps marching fast off the ridge towards the uproar. In fields towards Emmitsburg road, Longstreet's artillery presents an amazing sight. Alexander: "Every battery was limbered to the front, and the 2 batteries from the rear coming up, all 6 charged in line across the plain and went into action again at the position the enemy had deserted."

6 p.m. 1½ miles north of the main action, Lee gazes almost constantly through binoculars. Fremantle, at his H.Q., watches "the onward progress of the smoke . . ." Further north, from the Pennsylvania College outside town, Henry Berkeley is on "lookout for Yankee cavalry . . . By six o'clock all the atmosphere had become . . . like a thick fog, and I could only see the flash of the artillery . . ."

6 p.m. Thursday

Sickles's 1st division engulfed from peach orchard to Devil's Den. Meade, back on Cemetery Ridge, orders II corps' 1st division south in support. Federal crest swarming.

Confederates around the Den, Law's left flank, at storm centre. Bradfield, 1st Texas: "the fierce, angry shriek of shells . . . the hissing bullets, and their 'spat' as they struck . . . the leaping . . . from boulder to boulder of powder-begrimed men . . . I heard someone say, 'Here comes Barbee,' . . ." Through the smoke a galloping rider jumps to the ground, snatches a rifle and climbs a boulder. Staff Sgt. Barbee has left H.Q. to join the battle, "standing there, erect . . . firing—the wounded men below him passing up loaded guns . . ." Shot in both legs, he twice falls from the rock. "he crawled back a second time, but . . . wounded in the body, he again fell . . . crying and cursing . . ."

Southwards, other Texans and Alabamans, formation gone, forcing up Little Round Top piecemeal against Vincent's men. West: "we made sallies . . . over rocks and boulders and timber . . . It was more like Indian fighting than anything . . . They had sharp-shooters in trees . . ."

South again, Oates's regiments descending Big Round Top unopposed, "passed to the left-oblique entirely down the northern side . . ." Oates can see "Federal wagon-trains, and . . . ordnance wagons." It seems they are coming down behind the enemy's rear. Moving fast, Oates reaches the foot of the cliffs and detaches A com-

pany to surround the ammunition wagons.

6.10 p.m. S.W. of Little Round Top, Confederates still attacking heavily. 2 main assaults repulsed, a third of their men dead or wounded on the slope. 4th and 5th Texas and 48th Alabama begin crawling north, sheltered by high rocks along Plum Run, to try to out-flank Vincent's right.

WOODS AROUND WHEATFIELD

Federal V corps in action. Tilton's brigade forced back; Sweitzer's keeping line, ordered to retire across the field to peach orchard road at one end. General Caldwell rides up: his division of II corps "was driving the enemy in the woods" to the right, and needs support. Sweitzer's brigade again moves forward.

Confederates swarming among trees ahead are South Carolinans. Kershaw sees Sweitzer's advance: "a heavy column moved in two lines of battle across the wheat-field to attack my . . . 7th Regiment in flank . . ." He calls up the 15th, and Semmes's brigade from reserve. De Trobriand's brigade of Sickles's counter-attacks. Irregular lines, blue and grey, sway back and forth amid trampled wheat, scorched undergrowth, branches lopped by shell bursts. Fallen men, some screaming.

Barksdale's troops almost right through peach orchard. Northwards, Sickles's right flank under fire. Blake: "a kitten, mewing piteously . . . jumped upon the shoulders of one of the men . . ."

6.15 p.m. New grey battle lines, Wofford's brigade, surge forward.

LITTLE ROUND TOP

Alabamans, pressing uphill without skirmishers, hit the east tip of Vincent's position. From piled rocks, 20th Maine suddenly "poured into us the most destructive fire I ever saw", writes Oates. "Our line halted, but did not break . . . I could see through the smoke men . . . running from tree to tree back westward . . . I advanced my right, swinging it around . . ."

6.20. Chamberlain, 20th Maine: "Mounting a large rock, I was able to see . . . the enemy moving by the flank . . ." Nothing on his left but trees—and defenceless wagons. Firing continuously, half his men spread to twice their frontage, while others double back at right angles, beating Confederates by seconds. On Oates's left, 47th Alabama, paralysed by fire from 2 Federal regiments above, falls back.

Texans nearing position for renewed assault on west side of Little Round Top. Last of Federal V corps' 2nd division is crossing northern slopes towards wheatfield when 2 mounted officers are seen descending. Warren, having heard nothing, through the din, of Vincent's brigade below his crest while he watched the Confederate advance, is galloping for help. He shouts to Colonel O'Rorke to leave the column and bring up his 140th New York, on his authority, and gallops on himself for more troops or guns.

140th climb fast. Capt. Farley: "We . . . rushed along the wooded, rocky, eastern slope . . . the guns of Hazlett's battery . . . plunged directly through our ranks, the horses being urged to frantic efforts by the whips of their drivers and the cannoniers . . . at the wheels . . ."

6.30 p.m. 4th and 5th Texas and 48th Alabama make a last, furious charge. Major Rogers: "advanced boldly over the ground strewn with . . . their dead and dying comrades . . ." Vincent's right flank, 16th Michigan, is swamped. Above them, 140th New York surmounts the crest. Farley: "A great basin lay before us full of smoke and fire . . . riderless horses and fighting, fleeing and pursuing men . . . sulphurous fumes . . . wild cries . . . rattle of musketry, the booming of artillery . . . shrieks . . . The whole of Sickles's corps being slaughtered and driven . . ."

They see the 16th Michigan falling apart. Farley: "not a musket was loaded . . . The enemy were coming from our right . . ." In a second O'Rorke leaps from his saddle, shouts, "Down this way, boys," and the regiment, not stopping even to fix bayonets, rushes pell-mell for the enemy.

6.35 p.m. Wofford's Georgians emerge from peach orchard, clear now of Federals, just as Kershaw's men forced back to Rose's farm. Kershaw: "I saw Wofford riding at the head of his fine brigade, then coming in . . ."

6.35 p.m. Thursday

Federal reserves pouring in to wheatfield area: Cross's, Kelly's, Zook's brigades of II corps; now 2 brigades of regulars from V corps.

By Devil's Den 1st Texas clinging to their summit. Bradfield: "soon the long blue line came . . . up the valley . . . one officer, a major . . . rode a beautiful, high-spirited gray horse . . . As . . . his gallant men went down like grain . . . time and again . . . he rallied them . . . In the last . . . charge . . . riding into our very midst . . . horse and rider went down together . . ."

Out beyond the orchard, Sickles's lines crumbling fast. Battle now a savage, fragmented confusion. Alexander, with Longstreet's guns: "The artillery took part whenever it could, firing at everything in sight . . ."

Through trees, over loose rock, sweating gunners of 5th U.S. Battery D somehow get 6 pieces up Little Round Top. Lt. Hazlett killed, but his battery in action. On the hill's west face, Texans' final attack failed against fresh Federal reserves. Giles: "Major Rogers . . . mounted an old log . . . appealed . . . to 'stand fast.' . . . The balance of us had settled down behind rocks, logs and trees . . . John Haggerty . . . dashed up . . . saluted . . . and said: 'General Law presents his compliments and says hold the place at all hazards.' The major . . . shouted: 'Compliments, hell! . . . ask General Law if he expects me to hold the world in check with the 5th Texas . . .'"

From the Union centre, anxious generals watch the storm over peach orchard and Emmitsburg road swirling nearer. Sickles's corps seems in rout. Haskell: "Generals Hancock and Gibbon rode along the lines . . . at once cheer after cheer . . . rang out . . . for 'Hancock' and 'Gibbon' . . ."

6.40. Barksdale dead, his troops forcing on. Wofford's brigade joins the scattered remnants of Kershaw's, driving the woods north of wheatfield. Sweitzer's Federals outflanked: "my color-bearer, Ed. Martin, remarked, 'Colonel, I'll be damned if I don't think we are faced the wrong way; the rebs are up there in the woods behind us . . .'" No trace of divisional H.Q. Hard pressed on 3 sides, blue lines retreat across the exposed field, losing heavily. Houghton, 4th Michigan: "our Color Barrer was wounded . . . a Rebel grabed the flag . . . when our Colonel drew his revolver Shot the Rebel . . . a Rebel thrust a bayonet into the . . . Colonel . . . my tent mate James Johnston was shot . . . I herd Him Say I am Killed . . . the rest was groans . . ."

TROSTLE'S BARN

III corps H.Q. in chaos. Tremain finds Sickles, white faced, one leg smashed, against a wall: "a soldier . . . under the general's directions was buckling a saddle strap . . . above the knee" to staunch the bleeding.

Orderlies run for an ambulance while Sickles hands over to General Birney.

7 p.m. Second phase of Lee's attack: 2 right hand brigades, Willcox's and Perry's, of Hill's corps move off down the long slope towards Emmitsburg road. 2 Union batteries on the road tear gaps, but within minutes all Sickles's right is broken.

Meade piling in all reinforcements he can. Another brigade of II corps peels off the ridge south; 1st division of XII on its way from Culp's Hill "upon the double quick, leaping the stone walls" says Coffin. Haskell: "They formed lines of battle at the foot of the Taneytown road, and when the broken fragments of the 3rd Corps were swarming by . . . they came sweeping up, and with glorious old cheers, under fire, took their places on the crest . . ."

7.10. Confederates through the Emmitsburg road; charging uphill, battle flags red against a low sun. Haskell: "The whole slope . . . is full of them . . . in line, in column, and in masses . . . The battery men are ready . . . They drew the cords that moved the friction primers, and gun after gun, along the batteries . . . leaped where it stood and bellowed its canister. . .

"The roar of the discharges and the yells . . . pass unheeded; but the impassioned soul is all eyes . . . How madly the battery men are driving home the double charges of canister in those broad-mouthed Napoleons . . . Men are dropping . . . an arm dangling . . . a leg broken by a bullet, are limping and crawling towards the rear."

At 7.15 Wright's brigade of Hill's corps advances, routs last defenders from Emmitsburg road, pushes towards Cemetery Ridge.

LITTLE ROUND TOP

On crucial flank of whole Union army, soldiers from Maine and Alabama locked in combat. Oates's men dropping fast, his brother left dying. Oates: "waving my sword, shouting 'Forward . . .' . . . We drove the Federals . . . five times they rallied and charged us . . ." Alabama standard still flying. Another Maine charge "right up . . . hand to hand . . . A Maine man reached to grasp the staff of the colors when . . . Sgt. Pat O'Connor stove his bayonet through the head of the Yankee . . ."

For almost an hour the struggle has rolled "like a wave", says Chamberlain, 20th Maine. "The dead and wounded were now in front and then in our rear. . . . The intervals of the struggle were seized to remove our wounded . . . gather ammunition from . . . the field, and even to secure better muskets than the Enfields, which we found did not stand service well."

7.30 p.m. Thursday

CEMETERY RIDGE, GETTYSBURG

Lee's central attack sweeping all before it. Haskell: "The fire all along our crest is terrific . . . yet the madness of the enemy drove them on, clear up to the muzzle of the guns . . ."

Gibbon's 2nd division taking brunt of attack. Hancock, corps commander, gallops to Gibbon.

Wilcox's Alabaman brigade heading straight for thinnest part of Meade's line, south of Patterson's house. Above a narrow valley 8 companies of 1st Minnesota, 262 men, guarding a Federal battery. Through the murk Haskell sees "a flag dimly visible, coming towards us. . . ." Capt. Searles, 1st Minnesota: "the sun was setting as a great ball of fire . . . smoke had settled into the ravine, and the enemy's line disappeared down into the gloom . . ."

Lochren, nearby: "Hancock . . . rode up at full speed . . . calling out . . . 'What regiment is this?' '1st Minnesota' . . . 'Charge those lines!' commanded Han-

cock . . . in a moment . . . the regiment . . . with arms at 'right shoulder, shift' was sweeping down the slope . . ."

Marvin: "we went in on the charge the two armies wer not over 500 yds apart we had not fired a musket & the rebs wer fireing rappedly I dropped to the ground with a wound some whar I picked myself up as quick as possible when I saw blood on my shoe the heel of which was tore out I thought it a slight one & run to ketch up thinking that no rebel line could stand a charg of my Regt & if the Bayonet must be used I wanted a chance in as it was free to all."

Lochren: "silently, without orders . . . 'double-quick' had changed to utmost speed . . . with levelled bayonets . . . The 1st line broke . . . We then poured in our first fire . . ."

Marvin: "I had just ketched up again when I fell a second time to faint to get up I drank some watter & put some on my head and rists then I tried to walk to the

rear was to week for that so after resting again I tried the hands and knees"

Firing, bayoneting, clubbing, 262 men temporally stop a brigade of 1,800. At the end of the suicidal charge 215 from Minnesota lie dead or wounded.

LITTLE ROUND TOP

Without support, decimated, Oates's 15th Alabama can do no more. "my sergeant-major . . . reported that none of our troops were in sight, the enemy to be between us and the 4th Alabama, and swarming in the woods south . . ." Stoughton's U.S. Sharpshooters, lost during earlier retreat, now advancing towards the firing. Oates is told "two regiments were coming up behind . . . My dead and wounded . . . literally covered the ground. The blood stood in puddles . . ." Crawling officers relay Oates's order to prepare to run.

Higher up the ledge, 20th Maine, $\frac{1}{3}$ of their men casualties, also desperate. Chamberlain, hearing "a great roar of musketry in my rear", thinks he is surrounded. Ammunition exhausted. "My men were firing their last shot and getting ready to 'club' their muskets." Chamberlain sees one chance; orders "Fix bayonets!" A moment's hanging back, then Lt. Melcher leaps forward with upraised sword, colour-guard follows, and with a yell the regiment races downhill.

Simultaneously Oates signals 15th Alabama. "we ran like a herd of wild cattle, right through the line of dismounted cavalrymen. Some of the men as they ran seized three of the cavalrymen by the collars and carried them out prisoners. . . . Keils . . . had his throat cut by a bullet, and he ran past me breathing at his throat and the blood spattering."

7.40 p.m. Thursday

LITTLE ROUND TOP, GETTYSBURG

S.W. and W. slopes a stalemate. Texans hugging rocks, boulders, tree-stumps. "There seemed to be a viciousness in the very air . . ." says Giles. "We could hear the Yankee officer on the crest . . . cursing the men by platoons . . . Everything was on the shoot; no favors asked . . .

"My gun was so dirty that the ramrod hung in the barrel, and I could neither get it down nor out. I slammed the rod against a rock a few times and drove home ramrod, cartridge and all . . . ducked my head . . . and pulled the trigger. She roared like a young cannon and flew over my shoulder . . . It was no trouble to get another . . . The mountain side was covered with them.

"a little fellow from the 3rd Arkansas . . . behind a big stump . . . between biting cartridges and taking aim, he was singing at the top of his voice:

"'Now, let the wide world wag as it will,
I'll be gay and happy still.'"

All Federal guns salvaged from Sickles's corps massed on southern Cemetery Ridge; together with those on Little Round Top able now to concentrate on Devil's Den, bursting rock into jagged, lethal splinters. Colonel Work, 1st Texas: "Late in the evening a terrific fire of artillery . . . against . . . this regiment, many were killed and wounded, some losing their heads, and others so horribly mutilated . . . that their identity could hardly be established . . ."

Northwards, all wheatfield and its woods in Confederate hands. From both sides streams of wounded, on foot and stretcher, and, further back, ambulance wagons lurching over furrows. Houghton, 4th Michigan, is supporting his captain, trying to hobble. "He frequently had to stop . . . blood was gushing in His boots evry step . . . about one half mile east of little Roundtop we came to a 3d corps Hospital . . . in a Barn and Barn yard . . . a gard who informed us that they had about 300 wounded . . . and could not possibly admit any more the captain . . . layed down on the ground . . . The wounded were lying . . . in rows acrost the yard with Allies between for the waiters and Sergeons to pass through. . . . at the round tops clouds of smoke were rooling up as though a dozen Steam Engines were there at work . . . I took an alley . . . in to the Barn. . . . if I ever heard . . . groans it was there it was more than I could stand . . . the Captain . . . gave me His Sword and . . . I started out in Sarch of our Regiment"

3 hours after Law's first advance, Ewell's corps still waiting, in open fields, to make the final phase of Lee's grand assault. Johnson's division eastwards, Rodes's west of town. Leading Ewell's 1st division, under an ostrich hat-plume, swearing fluently, General Jubal Early. Finally, "a little before sunset", he gets orders to attack "as soon as Johnson should become engaged on my left", the noise of assault to be his signal.

A lone horseman is galloping with news for Johnson. Stuart's cavalry outriders at long last sighted on the York road. Johnson's exposed flanks should now be safe. Robert Stiles breasts a hill under shellfire, passes Johnson's shattered batteries, "hurled backward . . . by the very weight . . . of metal . . . guns dismounted . . . ammunition chests exploded . . . cannoneers with pistols . . . crawling around through the wreck shooting the struggling horses . . ."

CENTRE OF CEMETERY RIDGE

7.45 p.m. 3 minutes after sunset. Screaming like demons, Wright's Georgian brigade burst on to the crest near Meade's H.Q., capturing guns and men. Union centre breaks wide open. Meade, says his son, sees "the enemy making straight for the gap . . . He straightens himself in his stirrups . . . Suddenly some one cries out, 'There they come, General!' and, looking to the right, Newton is seen galloping in advance of Doubleday's division, followed by Robinson. In close column . . . the 2 divisions sweep down the Taneytown Road, swing around to the right, and as, amid the wildest excitement and shouting, they press forward to the line of battle, Meade rides ahead with the skirmish line, waving his hat, saying to those close about him, 'Come on, gentlemen'."

All Federal reserves used: all II corps, remnants of III, all V, 2 divisions of I, all but 1 brigade of XII, finally half of VI: some 50,000 Union men committed to battle.

Benton, with Lockwood's brigade: "we musicians . . . detailed as stretcher-bearers . . . orders kept coming . . . 'Faster',—'*Faster!*' . . . fences torn . . . trees cut . . . broken branches hanging . . . wounded men . . . dead men . . . a broken gun-carriage . . . a battery where the smoke-begrimed men were loading and firing across an open field, with the automatic movement . . . and . . . furious haste . . . as if they were on springs . . .

"A mounted officer . . . hard spurred . . . through the smoke . . . the incessant roar of rifles . . . the constant *th*, *th*, of bullets . . . before us . . . a long line of men in gray, firing continously. Our own line paused . . . then . . . a thousand jets of flame sprang from their front . . ."

After the furthest advance of the whole Confederate attack, a last failure in orders; no more troops move up to Wright's support; his brigade falls away before increasing numbers.

8 p.m. Survivors of 15th Alabama reclimbing Big Round Top. Company A, rejoined after failing to capture Union wagons, fighting as rearguards near mountain foot. Oates tries to reform his shattered regiment; faints himself; is carried to the summit.

3 miles N.E., beyond Rock Creek, Johnson has the news of Stuart's cavalry from Stiles, gives the long-awaited signal. His division begins to advance. Across ½ mile of cornfields, tree-studded Culp's Hill rises black against a deepening sky. Eastern slopes held by one Federal brigade in place of all XII corps—called off to reinforce Cemetery Ridge. General Greene's New York regiments spreading thinly into vacated trenches, trying to link right and left.

By 8.15 Johnson's leading troops, moving through shell-fire, slow at the first barrier. Lt. McKim: "Rock creek, waist-deep in some places, was waded. . . ." As skirmishers press uphill the racket of musketry echoes north; Early's division prepares to assault.

8.30 p.m. Thursday

NEW YORK CITY

175 miles from battle, the curtain falls on "The Little Treasure", opening playlet at Winter Garden Theatre, to polite cheers from a packed house. Mr. Floyd, dressed as Capt. Maydenblush, reappears out front with "a neat little speech". *Tribune*

A short interval, then a grotesque yokel "with a white face and an Irish dress" receives "a perfect *furore* of applause". The "Lover's Irish Drama . . . Handy Andy" proves "the event of the evening". Minstrel comedian Dan Bryant, discarding for once "the burnt cork and the bones", is irresistible.

BALTIMORE, MARYLAND

8.30 train steaming out from Philadelphia, Wilmington and Baltimore Railroad station has 6 Federal staff officers on board and a party of civilian mourners. Travelling freight, a wooden box encloses a metal coffin, painted like rosewood, draped with flags and flowers. Inside, the body of Meade's best general, John Reynolds, killed yesterday at Gettysburg. "The remains reached Baltimore on Thursday morning were at once taken to the embalmers . . ." writes his sister Jennie.

At Philadelphia tomorrow Ellie Reynolds can see little through the coffin window "The plate . . . much obscured . . . The face was swollen & one side bruised where he fell but it had been bleached . . . The moustache & beard had been cut very short . . . How I longed to see his hand!" A "little heart" around his neck and a ring marked "dear Kate" have already told their secret. Kate meets the family tomorrow; weeping by the coffin she confesses "they were to have been married after the war . . . They . . . were going to Europe . . ."

Some miles north of town, a wood burner rumbles over last crazy curves of Western Maryland Railroad, hauling extra cars loaded with soldiers in dirty grey, captured at Gettysburg. "At 9 o'clock . . . 800 prisoners . . . arrived at the Baltimore depot." *American*

Dispirited men progress slowly to prison camp. 2½ hours before *Tribune*'s correspondent writes: "11 o'clock p.m.—830 Rebel prisoners have just passed down Baltimore Street under guard. Among their number are General Archer and 70 other officers."

Somewhere south of Hanover Junction, loco *Tiger* cautiously returning along desolate Northern Central track towards Relay, outside Baltimore. "One of our engines proceeded . . . to within 7 miles of Gettysburg, where a burned bridge obstructed further progress. . . . heavy firing and much smoke towards Gettysburg." reports General Haupt. Construction engineer Clough, riding *Tiger*'s footplate, sending mounted men forward to inspect the line, has counted "19 bridges destroyed between York Haven and Hanover Junction", and on the Gettysburg branch "2 smaller ones gone". Haupt, getting the report at midnight, at Relay, sends "half of my bridge corps with train . . . via Baltimore and Philadelphia, to work south, the other half to work north." Apart from Confederate destruction, a shaky track with 300 ft radius curves, too acute for flanged wheels of ordinary locos, holds poor prospects. Haupt warns Washington "not much dependence can be placed upon" it.

RICHMOND, VIRGINIA

Along defence perimeter, militia and volunteers begin a night in open trenches. Shops and offices closed all day. Attacked an hour ago, Keyes deserting Baltimore Cross Roads. "Yankees . . . driven back to White House." signals General D. H. Hill at 11 p.m.

Nearly 200 miles inland, Andersonville shows no sign yet of coming horror. By next year's end, some 28,000 Union prisoners will be huddled within a bare 25 acre stockade, straining brown sewage through shirts to drink, starving. Prescott Tracy will testify on release: "average of deaths . . . at the time I left . . . was over 130 a day. . . . In some cases the inner edges of the 2 bones of the arms . . . with the intermediate blood vessels, were plainly visible when held towards the light."

THE SOUTH

Sun set 25 minutes ago in New Orleans. Vital river city, entry port for the Mississippi, under northern occupation. With Confederate forces inland short of supplies, Union officers search all steamer baggage for contraband. Grace King's mother, on disembarking upriver, found extra flour barrels among her luggage. "Hush", whispers the captain, "I am a Confederate." Carried ashore, flour revealed smuggled drugs.

Dark streets to the levee are quiet tonight. Federal H.Q. has rumours that ships bound upstream may be used as raiders; today's orders: "no steamer . . . allowed to pass . . . except by special authority." A guard ship watches the parapet. Town club rooms and gambling dens choking to cigar smoke for the last time during crisis, tomorrow closed by martial law.

Peaceful, garrison routine at Beaulieu, near Savannah. Georgia Light Artillery "painting the Carriages and Limbers" today, despite "slight showers". Private Fenley stumbles in after a day's absence "(being out in the woods gambling, I suspect) was placed in the Bomb-proof at night." *Capt. Hanleiter's diary*

On St. Helena Island, towards Charleston, Colonel Shaw is being entertained at a plantation "shout" of Negro songs. In 16 days he will die on the parapet of Fort Wagner, his Federal Negro regiment, 54th Massachusetts, shot to pieces beside him.

Capt. Higginson, with 1st South Carolina, also Federal and Negroes, on the same island. Like many a Northerner, Higginson succumbs to the magic of the South: "among the endless flowering forests . . . as I rode along our outer lines . . . and watched the glimmering flames which . . . starred the opposite river-shore, the longing was irresistible to cross the barrier of dusk . . . to glide along, noiselessly paddling, with a dusky guide, through the . . . marshes, scaring the reed-birds, which wailed and fled away into the darkness . . ."

71

8.40 p.m. Thursday

CULP'S HILL, GETTYSBURG

Capt. Jones, 60th New York: "the woods were all flecked with . . . flashes . . ." Union skirmishers driven from tree to tree up towards their entrenchments. Thin line of Greene's brigade, "nervous fingers" on triggers, waiting.

McKim, below the Confederate advance, listens as "volley after volley . . . re-echoed among the hills. I felt very anxious about our boys in front . . ." He asks permission to lead up the reserves. Amid trees, in growing darkness, rifle flashes show no direction and firing becomes almost blind. 1st North Carolina begins shooting its own brigade.

Just outside town, Hays's Louisiana regiments have lain all day in fields astride a stream, suffering shell-fire, and the stink of Winebrenner's tannery. As musketry swells on Culp's Hill, couriers gallop from H.Q. Early: "I ordered Hays and Avery to advance . . . and Gordon . . . to support . . ."

9 p.m. Wainwright, with Federal batteries on Cemetery Hill, sees columns approaching under a risen moon. His guns open. At the hill's foot, Hays's men form quickly for the charge. Wainwright: "we commenced firing canister, depressing the guns more and more . . . smoke lay so thick that you could not see ten yards

ahead . . ." Hays's Louisiana "Tigers", "exposed to a most terrific fire", furiously clear a stone wall, carry a second, then "Still advancing . . . an abatis of fallen timber and . . . rifle pits. This line we broke . . ."

Germans of Union XI corps fleeing in droves. Wainwright says one of his battery lieutenants "stretched his men along the road, with fence rails! to try to stop the runaways . . ."

9.30. Louisianans only feet from apex of whole Federal position. One last screaming rush to the summit, capturing "4 stands of colours", and they are among the guns. General Schurz: "suddenly a tremendous turmoil at Wiedrich's and Ricketts' batteries . . ." He orders off 2 nearest regiments who fix bayonets on the run. He fights his way through "a rushing crowd" of broken men to find "at the Batteries . . . an indescribable scene . . . rebel infantry had scaled the breastworks . . . the cannoneers defended themselves desperately . . . with hammers and fence rails, handspikes and stones . . ." A Confederate officer, sword lifted, claims Wiedrich's guns: "This battery is ours!" A German from Buffalo fells him with a sponge staff: "No, dis battery is *unser*!"

Hays's Tigers, fighting savagely, take the edge of the

72

cemetery. Even now, as before on the ridge, captured guns could sweep Meade's whole position. But again no support. Darkness is torn by a sheet of fire, and 14th Indiana leads an entire Federal brigade of veteran II corps up at the double. Charged by new lines, Hays orders retreat to a wall below the hill.

Somewhere behind, Early rides to find why Rodes has not advanced, is told no orders reached Pender's division to support Rodes's right. But messages of Hays's withdrawal mean it is now too late.

10 p.m. After 3 assaults and repulses, through a hail of bullets stripping foliage, chipping trees, Johnson's troops on Culp's Hill seize a line of trenches from 149th New York. Federal reinforcements block further advance, firing peters out. In full darkness both sides lie by their rifles, in places lines only yards apart.

Battle subsiding everywhere. Jacob sees some of Ewell's men back in town: "The Rebels returned again to our street at 10 p.m., and prepared their supper." 3 miles south, Meade's left flank is safe. Vincent lies dying, but his brigade, with 2 more from V corps, holds Little Round Top. After clearing the valley, Chamberlain's 200 survivors of 20th Maine, reforming, silently "pressed up the mountain side in very extended order"

to Big Round Top's summit, surprising 25 of Oates's rearguard.

In fields southwards, Oates, who has ordered full retreat, sees his 15th Alabama crawl in for a bitter roll-call; "223 enlisted men answered", and only 19 officers, out of 500 who began the attack.

Across 5 miles of trampled earth, thousands upon thousands lie dead or wounded, in gulleys to escape shell-bursts, helpless in the open, in rude "hospitals". On Cemetery Ridge, writing a crabbed copperplate, Matthew Marvin stoically completes his diary: "about 10 o'clock the Ambulances come & took us to the rear I have got about all the pain I can stand Weather Am Lowery Pm pleasant".

Texans pinned to scarred slopes of Little Round Top. John West: "Just in front . . . open space on rising ground . . . About 10 o'clock . . . Goldsticker of Company A ventured out. He was mortally wounded. I can hear his plaintive cry, 'Water! water! Great God, bring me water!' . . ."

Night

Both armies keep uneasy position. Appalling casualties have produced only stalemate. But battle on this scale cannot last much longer, men on both sides sense to-morrow will be decisive. Either Lee will be on the road to Washington, or retreating, beaten, to the Potomac. The weakened Confederacy can never hope to mount another invasion of the North; this is the last throw.

A candle, stuck in its wax, gutters in the front room of the Leister cottage. In a space "not more than 10 or 12 ft square", all Meade's corps commanders, summoned to H.Q., crowd around a small pinewood table. Some standing, 3 or 4 on wooden chairs, Warren—wounded—asleep on a bed, a water bucket and tin cup in a corner. The generals talk while Meade listens. Worried by his losses—strength returns list only 58,000 men in line—miles from main supplies, he knows how narrowly his army has escaped disaster. One false move now could lose the campaign, even the war. And, discounting Antietam, Lee has never yet been beaten.

Eventually 3 questions are written out, everyone answers in turn. Should the army 1. Remain in position? 2. If so, should it attack? 3. If not, how long await attack? No one thinks the army fit to attack; all agree with Slocum: "Stay and fight it out."

As they leave, towards midnight, Meade turns thoughtfully to Gibbon, remarking that since Lee has failed on both flanks, if he does attack tomorrow "it will be *in your front*." Hancock, Newton and Gibbon "crawling into the H.Q. ambulance" parked under peach trees behind II corps, snatch a few hours sleep.

A mile west, Lee, alone with his staff, planning, preparing. Reasons for today's failures seem clear: ignorance of enemy movements due to lack of cavalry, Longstreet's slowness, poor co-ordination between corps. The incomparable Army of Northern Virginia is still a fighting unit; once properly concentrated, Lee believes its hardened veterans, in one supreme effort, must

surely prevail.

Ewell will re-attack at dawn; a bombardment heavier than anything yet seen will smother the Federal ridge; Longstreet's corps will smash Meade's left centre, cutting the enemy in two. Couriers ride away with orders.

Clouds hiding a full moon. Artillery silent, gun barrels sponged, teams stretched by the wheels. Occasional picket fire; infantry huddled behind breastworks, in the open, wherever battle left them. Slopes littered with haversacks, clothing, human fragments, smoking rubbish. Across the dark landscape, lanterns; the slow rattling of ambulances among the dead and wounded. Blake sees volunteers carrying water canteens into no-man's-land, bring back men on blankets and fence rails.

Behind the Federal crest, Coffin hears the "rumble of artillery . . . of ammunition and supply wagons going up . . . Lights were gleaming in the hollows, beneath the shade of oaks and pines, where the surgeons were at work . . ." McKim hears guns moving all night on to Culp's Hill, mistakenly thinks the Federals are retreating. Near the Emmitsburg road some of Longstreet's batteries taking new positions. Alexander hard at work: "horses were to be fed and watered, those killed . . . replaced from the wagon teams, ammunition . . . replenished . . ." Northwards, the "Lady of Gettysburg" writes her diary: "just finished washing a few pieces for my child, for we expect to be compelled to leave town tomorrow, as the Rebels say it will most likely be shelled."

Both armies strengthening defences. On Devil's Den, and along the stony Round Tops, men cannot entrench, instead pile boulders and chippings into breastworks. Law: "all through the night we could hear them at work as the rocks were dropped in place . . ."

Friday 3 July

4 a.m. "Boom! Boom! Two guns, deep and heavy, at 4 o'clock . . . flashes from all the hills—" writes Coffin. Confederates on Culp's Hill, shaken awake by a murderous bombardment at 500 yards range, discover Union artillery has far from retreated. Johnson's guns cannot be dragged up the steep slope, have "no means of replying", writes McKim. Slocum's XII corps have returned to hold the hill in strength; as dawn breaks they attack. Incessant volleys and shell-fire strip the trees; Confederates rise from their trenches to counter-attack. Heavy fighting spreads.

Off the Emmitsburg road, Alexander at work again since 3. Washington Artillery battalion now up with 10 more guns. At 5, Pickett's Virginian division, halted last evening on the Cashtown road, resumes its march. By 7, they reach Longstreet's left, and form battle lines on reverse slopes of Seminary Ridge. Arms stacked; men rest. John Dooley, 1st Virginia: "we amuse ourselves by pelting each other with green apples."

Across the valley, Lee rides to Longstreet, who yet again has not stirred. Longstreet argues that McLaws's and Hood's broken divisions can barely hold their own, let alone assault. Lee finally agrees that Longstreet shall use only Pickett's fresh division, replacing his 2 others by 2 from Hill, and shift therefore axis of attack northwards, to strike the centre of Cemetery Ridge. Orders amended, troops again on the move. Meade's prophesy proving correct . . .

On Culp's Hill, Johnson's soldiers make a last all-out attempt, suffer staggering losses, retire beaten to the foot. With Slocum's XII corps firmly back in their own trenches, battles ceases. Ewell's attack ended before Longstreet's even begun.

By noon, sun burning a brilliant sky. Haskell: "not a sound of a gun or musket . . . The army lolls and longs for the shade . . ."

Confederate artillery, 74 guns of Longstreet, plus 60 of Hill, stretch ¾ mile north from peach orchard along Emmitsburg road and on slopes behind. Behind Seminary Ridge 10 brigades from 3 divisions waiting: some 15,000 infantry. Many boys: Pickett's Virginians average 19 years.

Longstreet has ridden the length of the line with Lee, deeply pessimistic, but finalising instructions to separate units. Direction of attack to be aimed at a copse of trees prominent on the crest. Alexander is detailed to judge when the bombardment has silenced Federal artillery, or achieved maximum effect, then advise Pickett to advance.

1 p.m. Stillness broken by 2 guns. Within seconds, massed salvoes send shells exploding non-stop along Union crest. Meade's H.Q. an inferno, abandoned. Correspondent Samuel Wilkeson: "As many as 6 in a second, constantly 2 in a second, bursting and screaming . . . in the yard . . . hitched horses . . . reared and plunged . . . 16 lay dead and mangled . . . still fastened by their halters . . ." Crounze, at the cemetery: "fences . . . flew in splinters . . . earth, torn up in clouds, blinded the eyes . . ." Wilkeson spies "an ambulance driven . . . at full speed . . . horse . . . on 3 legs. A hinder one . . . shot off at the hock . . . soldiers . . . torn to pieces . . . not a straggler to be seen . . ."

Federal guns replying. Gibbon sees under "a heavy pall of smoke" only artillerymens' legs as they work the guns. Haskell: "shells bursting in the air . . . a bright gleam of lightning radiating from a point . . ." ½ mile away, Benton numbed by "a continuous roar . . . the air seemed . . . paralysed. . . . An ammunition wagon rumbled heavily . . . a . . . courier galloped past . . . hoofs striking fire . . . but to us they were silent . . ."

Longstreet's guns firing high: Union batteries taking more casualties than infantry on forward slopes. Minutes, an hour, an eternity passes. 250 guns belching a mile long strata of smoke. Men have never dreamed such shell-fire possible. Confederate assault troops helpless, face down, under falling trees and splinters of intense return bombardment. Hundreds killed or wounded where they lie.

2.50 p.m. Alexander has seen some of Meade's batteries retire. Ammunition almost gone, Confederate guns cease; then Union. Throughout 47 southern regiments, shouted commands: "Fall in!" David Johnston hears Pickett crying "Up men . . . Don't forget today that you are from old Virginia!" He sees men pass through the ranks of wounded—like himself—calling "Good-bye, boys! Goodbye!" Through clearing smoke, Federals watch column after column, flag after flag, emerge from the woods, and halt to align ranks. 6 brigades, in 2 wings, form nearly a mile of frontage, 5 support brigades in rear.

Fresh Federal batteries replace those withdrawn. On the silent crest Haskell hears "the clicking of the iron axles as the guns were rolled up by hand . . ."

A long, strange hush, as 15,000 assault troops correct their lines. Then, as though on parade, flags red in the sun, a massive, steady march forward. Over fields, over fences, across the Emmitsburg road; converging, climbing uphill, closing great gaps torn by Federal guns blazing with canister. Ground behind thickening with fallen, crawling, dying. Near the crest, blue-coat infantry pour in crippling volleys; Confederates halt to reply; whole regiments become trapped in cross-fire. Men dropping fast, some hundreds cross the last wall and reach the trees, cutting and clubbing among the guns. But losses are too high; against ever increasing Union reserves and a blizzard of fire, Virginians and Carolinans, mere remnants of regiments, stagger back across the smoking valley. The grand attack has failed.

Lee, controlling his distress, rides among the survivors, encouraging each: "All this will come right in the end . . . We want all good men and true men just now." Every brigade is wrecked; Pickett's division has lost nearly 3,000 men. Of all the assault troops, less than half return. Defence lines reform on Seminary Ridge while Alexander's gunners prepare for expected counter-attack. But Federals are exhausted too; Meade makes no move.

11 p.m. At new Union H.Q., Coffin finds "a dark forest, —the evening breeze gently rustling the green leaves . . . locusts singing . . . bivouac fires glimmering . . ." Among his generals, "Meade stooping, weary, his slouched hat laid aside . . . 'Bully! bully! bully all round!' said he . . ."

Beyond the valley, General Imboden, at Lee's H.Q., sees Lee painfully dismount: "He threw his arm across his saddle to rest himself, and . . . leaned . . . motionless as a statue." Imboden breaks silence: "General, this has been a hard day on you."

Slowly, face set in grief, Lee talks of success so nearly gained. "I never saw troops behave more magnificently than Pickett's . . ."

Then, in agonized tones: "Too bad! *Too bad*! Oh! Too bad!"

After

For Lee, nothing remains but retreat. Artillery without reserve ammunition; 20,486 men killed, wounded, missing; a hostile countryside stripped of food and forage; an impregnable enemy position. His only hope is to drag his shattered columns over the mountain passes and recross the Potomac into Virginia before Meade's counter-attack brings total disaster. The moment they are ready, trains of wounded will be escorted by Imboden's cavalry, infantry marching after by corps, Ewell's as rearguard.

Federal losses even higher: 23,049 when finally counted. Again lanterns guide ambulances and stretchers over the ghastly slopes; worst wounded linger through a second night. Surgeons, at corps' hospitals, cut and prod and sew. Marvin now moved under some trees: "old leaves mad the beds with sticks or stones for pillows we wer all rite at last"

Reid and Coffin ride out with their stories; in Washington before midnight Lincoln watches the first victory telegram click into the War Department: correspondent Homer Byington has arranged an exclusive line from Hanover via Baltimore, giving New York's *Tribune* a fantastic coup.

Saturday, Lee's infantry guard their lines while wounded are gathered along Chambersburg road. Meade still refuses to risk attack. Everywhere the scorched, sweet smell of powder and putrifying flesh; some blackening corpses 3 days old. Burial parties begin. For comrades, single graves. Houghton, in wheatfield woods: "blankets . . . torn into . . . a roll . . . under Each ones Head then blankets was spread over them . . . so no dirt could not tuch them." Unknown enemy heaped in common trenches, a red chalked sign above, "75 Rebels buried here", "54 Rebs there", says Haskell.

By afternoon, blinding rain and wind set in. In Federal hospitals in exposed fields, amputated limbs heaped in mounds. Schurz: "Most of the operating tables . . . in the open where the light was best . . . partially protected . . . by tarpaulins." Gettysburg churches, many houses, taken. Berkeley, searching northwards for water, finds "Every house, shed, barn and hut was filled with wounded, dying . . . Blood everywhere."

Except for morphine, surgery is Napoleonic. Bound stumps are kept wet to bring out "laudable puss"; nitric acid poured on resultant gangrene. Germs kill more than bullets.

Before nightfall, 17 miles of Confederate wagons, hoods streaming water, with bare floorboards and unsprung wheels, lurch off on a nightmare of torture. Lee's wounded, screaming at every jolt, blaspheming, imploring someone to shoot them, dragged without chance of halt or aid. Wounded prisoners scarcely better. Dooley, shot 30 yards from Meade's guns, "sans tents, sans blanket, sans fires, sans water, sans everything . . ." Fouled drinking water brings delirium. "I'm proud I belong to the 1st Virginia . . ." repeats one boy over and over.

Hill's corps moves off during darkness; Longstreet's starts at dawn. Sunday afternoon Ewell's rearguard crosses the desolate valley and takes the Fairfield road.

While Union engineers race to repair tracks of the Northern Central and Hanover lines, Westminster

remains nearest railhead. Sunday morning 3 wagons of medicines and food have come up, off-loaded from rail car at Westminster, sent by Sanitary Commission at Washington on first battle news. Women nurses arrive. Emily Souder finds "Chloride of lime . . . freely used in the broad streets . . ."

Monday sees more wagons; Tuesday the railroad opens as far as a temporary station 2 miles E. of town, where transit camps shelter wounded awaiting trains to Baltimore.

Monday Lee's advanced columns reached Williamsport, to find bridges destroyed and the Potomac, swollen by rains, unfordable. Defence perimeters are dug while the miles of wounded begin crossing in ferry boats; engineers tear up wood for new bridges; Imboden's and Stuart's cavalry hold off Federal raiders. Almost no food for 3 days. Berkeley: "nothing to eat, except wheat which we rubbed out of its heads in our hands . . ." Morale still high: Fremantle hears men ridiculing a picture of Lincoln: "Come out of that hat —I know you're in it—I sees your legs a-dangling down."

Meade seems paralysed, not until 12 July surrounding the bridgehead. Before he finally attacks on the 14th, Lee's army is crossing, wading flood waters down to 4 feet, fighting a desperate rearguard over swaying pontoons.

Invasion's end. The North is jubilant; for the first time the Army of the Potomac has won. Meade becomes famous, although Lincoln is bitterly disappointed that Lee's escape will lengthen the war.

Gettysburg slowly returns to life. Pennsylvania, with 17 Northern States, builds a cemetery for Union dead; horse carcasses still lie when, on 19 November, huge crowds witness its dedication. Parades, salutes, 2 hours' oratory; spectators already drifting away when Lincoln rises. He holds 2 handwritten sheets. "Silly, flat, and dishwatery", thinks the *Chicago Times*. "ludicrous . . . dull and commonplace", sneers London's *Times*. 266 words read in a flattish voice; hardly anyone remarks the last 17: "that government of the people, by the people, for the people, shall not perish from the earth."

The Union is saved. Vicksburg's surrender cuts the Confederacy in two; the Army of Northern Virginia has made its last invasion. Valour and tactics are powerless against lack of food, of men, of guns; against siege and blockade. War rages almost 2 more years before Lee surrenders 28,231 starving survivors to Grant at Appomattox. On 12 April 1865, Chamberlain, General now, calls Federal troops to attention alongside the road, rifles shouldered in salute. Battle flags dipped, an army in rags marches past, rifles at the slope. "not a sound . . . not a cheer, nor word nor motion of man, but awful stillness . . ." writes Chamberlain.

In strict rank regiment after regiment lays down arms. Rifles stacked, colours draped across, cartridge boxes burned. Lee's veterans, paroled, are soldiers no more. The next day Chamberlain sees "the hillsides were alive with men . . . making their way as by the instinct of an ant . . . for his own little harbor or home.

"And we were left alone. . . ."

Acknowledgements

The author wishes to thank those organizations which have given him invaluable help in tracing information and manuscript sources, and in particular the following:

Bureau of Topographic and Geologic Survey, Harrisburg, Pennsylvania.
Franklin and Marshall College.
H.M. Nautical Almanac Office, Royal Greenwich Observatory.
Louisiana State University, Department of Archives.
Massachusetts Historical Society.
Minnesota Historical Society, Manuscripts Department.
State of Mississippi, Department of Archives and History.
University of Michigan, Library. Michigan Historical Collections.
University of North Carolina, Library. Southern Historical Collection.
University of Texas, Library.

The author gratefully acknowledges his debt to the following publications:

NEWSPAPERS. British Museum. Colindale.
OFFICIAL RECORDS, WAR OF THE REBELLION. U.S. War Department. Washington. 1889–1911.
SOUTHERN HISTORICAL SOCIETY PAPERS. Richmond.
THE REBELLION RECORD. 1861–8. New York.
BATTLES AND LEADERS. 1887, edited by R. U. Johnson.
THE PHOTOGRAPHIC HISTORY OF THE CIVIL WAR, edited by F. T. Miller. 1911.
Amory K. Allen: Letters reprinted in INDIANA MAGAZINE OF HISTORY.
Charles E. Benton: AS SEEN FROM THE RANKS. G. P. Putnam. 1902.
Henry Robinson Berkeley: DIARY—FOUR YEARS IN THE CONFEDERATE ARTILLERY, edited by William H. Runge for the Virginia Historical Society. University of Virginia Press. 1961.
Henry N. Blake: THREE YEARS IN THE ARMY OF THE POTOMAC. Lee and Shepard. 1865.
Chauncey H, Cooke: Letters in WISCONSIN MAGAZINE OF HISTORY. State Historical Society of Wisconsin. Vol. IV. 1920–1.
Kate Cumming: KATE, edited by Richard Barksdale Harwell. Lousiana State University Press. 1959.
James A. Connolly: THREE YEARS IN THE ARMY OF THE CUMBERLAND, edited by Paul M. Angle. Indiana University Press. 1959.
Sylvia Dannett: NOBLE WOMEN OF THE NORTH. Thomas Yoseloff. 1959.
John W. De Forest: A VOLUNTEER'S ADVENTURES, edited by James H. Croushore. Yale University Press. 1946.
John Dooley: A CONFEDERATE SOLDIER, HIS WAR JOURNAL, edited by J. T. Durkin. University of Notre Dame Press, Indiana. 1963.
A. Fremantle: THREE MONTHS IN THE SOUTHERN STATES. William Blackwood and Sons, Edinburgh. 1863.
Josiah Gorgas: THE CIVIL WAR DIARY, edited by Frank E. Vandiver. University of Alabama Press. 1947.
C. R. Hanleiter: Diary published in ATLANTA HISTORICAL BULLETIN. Atlanta Historical Society.
Frank A. Haskell: THE BATTLE OF GETTYSBURG. The Mudge Press. 1908.
Isaac V. Heard: HISTORY OF THE SIOUX WAR. Harper and Brothers. 1864.

Thomas W. Higginson: ARMY LIFE IN A BLACK REGIMENT. Michigan State University Press. 1960.
Jacob Hoke: THE GREAT INVASION. W. J. Shuey. 1887.
Michael Jacobs: NOTES ON THE REBEL INVASION. J. B. Lippincott and Co. 1864.
David E. Johnston: THE STORY OF A CONFEDERATE BOY IN THE CIVIL WAR. Glass and Prudhomme. 1914.
Robert G. Kean: INSIDE THE CONFEDERATE GOVERNMENT, edited by Edward Younger. Oxford University Press, New York. 1957.
Grace King: MEMOIRS OF A SOUTHERN WOMAN OF LETTERS. Macmillan, New York. 1932.
A Lady of Gettysburg: Diary quoted in THE UNION READER, edited by Richard B. Harwell. Longmans Green. 1958.
A Lady of Virginia: DIARY OF A SOUTHERN REFUGEE. E. J. Hale. 1868.
William Lochren: THE FIRST MINNESOTA AT GETTYSBURG address. Reprinted in GLIMPSES OF THE NATION'S STRUGGLE by Commanderie of the Military Order of the Loyal Legion, Minnesota. 1893.
Armistead L. Long: MEMOIRS OF R. E. LEE. Sampson Low. 1886.
Randolf H. McKim: A SOLDIER'S RECOLLECTIONS. Longmans Green. 1910.
George Meade: LIFE AND LETTERS OF GEORGE GORDON MEADE. Charles Scribner's Sons. 1913.
Oliver W. Norton: THE ATTACK AND DEFENCE OF LITTLE ROUND TOP. Neale Publishing Company. 1913.
Robert D. Patrick: RELUCTANT REBEL, THE SECRET DIARY OF ROBERT PATRICK, edited by F. Jay Taylor. Louisiana State University Press. 1959
David D. Porter: INCIDENTS AND ANECDOTES OF THE CIVIL WAR. Appleton and Co. 1885.
James T. Ramer: NARRATIVE OF THE 7TH REGIMENT in MINNESOTA IN THE CIVIL AND INDIAN WARS. St Paul. 1891.
Fitzgerald Ross: A VISIT TO THE CITIES AND CAMPS OF THE CONFEDERATE STATES. William Blackwood and Sons. 1865.
Royal D. Ross: JOURNAL printed in COLLECTIONS OF STATE HISTORICAL SOCIETY OF NORTH DAKOTA. VOL II. Bismark. 1908.
Carl Schurz: REMINISCENCES. John Murray. 1909.
Robert Stiles: FOUR YEARS UNDER MARSE ROBERT. Neale Publishing Company. New York. 1903.
Katherine Stone: BROKENBURN, edited by John B. Anderson. Louisiana State University Press.
Prescott Tracey: Deposition before Committee of Inquiry of U.S. Sanitary Commission, 1864, published in NARRATIVE OF PRIVATIONS AND SUFFERINGS OF U.S. SOLDIERS WHILE PRISONERS OF WAR . . . Washington.
Henry E. Tremain: TWO DAYS OF WAR. Bonnell, Silver and Bowers. 1905.
Charles S. Wainwright: A DIARY OF BATTLE, edited by Allan Nevins. Harcourt Brace and World. 1962.
Gideon Welles: DIARY. Houghton Mifflin Company. 1911.
Walt Whitman: SPECIMEN DAYS. 1882.
Walt Whitman: Letters to his mother, in THE COLLECTED WRITINGS OF WALT WHITMAN: THE CORRESPONDENCE, edited by Edwin H. Miller. New York University Press. 1961.
John A. Wyeth: WITH SWORD AND SCALPEL. Harper and Brothers. 1914